Meaning in Life

Sarvananda

indhorse Publications

Published by
Windhorse Publications Ltd.
38 Newmarket Road
Cambridge
CB5 8DT, UK
email: info@windhorsepublications.com
www.windhorsepublications.com

© Sarvananda 2009

First Edition 2009

Cover design by Peter Wenman
Cover image © Windhorse Publications Ltd.
Printed by Bell & Bain Ltd., Glasgow

British Library Cataloguing in Publication Data:
A catalogue record for this book is available from the British Library

ISBN: 9781 899579 87 7
ISSN 2041 - 2509

As this work is not of a scholarly nature, Pali and Sanskrit words have been
transliterated without their diacritical marks.

Poem on p.65 from *One Robe, One Bowl: The Zen Poetry of Ryokan*,
translated by John Stevens, © 1977, Weatherhill Books.
Reprinted by arrangement with Shambhala Publications Inc., Boston MA.
www.shambhala.com

Contents

About the Author

Sarvananda (Alastair Jessiman) was born and educated in Glasgow. In 1987, after being ordained as a member of the Western Buddhist Order, he moved to Norwich where, over the last twenty years, he has taught classes in Buddhism and meditation. At present he earns a living by writing and has had six plays and a comedy series, *Boxer and Doberman*, broadcast on BBC Radio. He is also the education officer for the Norwich Buddhist Centre and has a particular interest in meditation.

Acknowledgements

I'd like to thank Jinamitra, Sagaraghosa and Caroline of Windhorse Publications for their help and encouragement, and for suggesting the book in the first place. Satyadaka read the earlier drafts and contributed a lot of ideas and advice. And some of my late night conversations with Jinavamsa have found their way into chapter 7. Many thanks to them all.

Dedication

In writing this book, and considering the theme of meaning in life, I've been made even more aware of how much I owe to my teacher, Sangharakshita. This book is dedicated to him with much gratitude and admiration.

Introduction:
Questions! Questions!

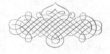

More than at any other time in history, mankind faces a crossroads. One path leads to despair and utter hopelessness. The other, to total extinction. Let us pray we have the wisdom to choose correctly. I speak, by the way, not with any sense of futility, but with a panicky conviction of the absolute meaninglessness of existence which could easily be interpreted as pessimism. [1]

WOODY ALLEN'S 'MY SPEECH TO THE GRADUATES' was published in a collection of his comic pieces in 1980, about the time I graduated from university. As a philosophy of life it left me pretty unequipped for the rough and tumble in store, but it was a philosophy which had resonated with me, to a great extent, ever since I'd been a child.

'What's the point of cutting the grass anyway?' I asked my heavily perspiring Mummy on one occasion. 'It's only going to grow again.'

My mother laughed but, significantly, failed to answer the question. I tended to ask a lot of questions as a little boy, questions to which my parents very patiently attempted to respond. A lot of the questions concerned death. From the age of five, I was seriously worried about death. I would lie in bed listening to my heart beat and ponder the fragility of my life. The anxiety this provoked would make my heart beat faster - and faster - and convince me that I was having a heart attack. Even if my heart didn't stop beating *now*, one day it *would* stop beating and I would be dead, I reflected. What was the point of living if it was all going to end in death?

I remember watching a nature programme with my two cousins (who were twins). They would have been about six at the time. I was a year older. During the programme, the camera settled on the face of a dead deer.

'What's wrong with the deer?' asked Lindsay.

'It's dead,' I said brutally.

'That poor deer,' said Neal.

'We all *die*,' I said, with all the world-weariness of a death-obsessed seven-year-old.

I'll never forget the twins' reaction. They looked at me, and then at one another, and, at exactly the same moment, they burst into tears and were inconsolable for hours.

'Alastair, what did you say to the twins?'

'I didn't say anything! I just said we were going to *die!*'

The twins' grief was deep and terrible, and the incident (which invested me, by the way, with a certain sense of power) became etched on my mind. Upon every life, even upon the life of every child, death casts its inevitable pall.

What's the point of cutting the grass if it's only going to grow again? What's the point of living if we're only going to die? Does life have any meaning? Or can it be simply and concisely summed up in Samuel Beckett's image of a woman giving birth over an open grave?

It was in my student days that such questions began to become really pressing. Impatient for certainties, in the face of these questions, I found the tolerant smile and the gentle shrug of the agnostic unhelpful and irritating. The writers and artists who excited me at university were those who responded to the Big Questions with confidence, or at least passion.

There was the Victorian poet James Thomson, for example, who in *The City of Dreadful Night* evoked a nightmare vision of a meaningless universe utterly indifferent to human affairs. The city in his poem was a place of alienation and spiritual despair, and I particularly thrilled to the description of the strange figure with 'steadfast and intolerable eyes' who climbed the pulpit and delivered an anti-sermon in a city cathedral. With a kind of unholy joy, this strange minister announced to the congregation, slumped and scattered below, that there was no God. 'No Fiend with names divine/ Made us and tortures us.'[2]

'There is no God.' It felt very liberating reading these words spoken so starkly, without apology or qualification. Was it true? Thomson's dark and uncompromising vision certainly excited me but the poem was a hymn of despair. To live, not just without God, but without any meaning in life at all, seemed an unbearable prospect.

William Wordsworth offered me a very different kind of conviction regarding the meaning of life. For Wordsworth, meaning was to be found in 'the visionary power of Nature'.[3] *The Prelude*, Wordsworth's long poem about his younger self, described the growth of his mind and poetic sensibility, and how his sympathies were enlarged by contact with Nature. The poem's images of the young boy, rowing on a lake or skating or wandering the hills until sunset, somehow seemed to resonate with me, although I was a child of the suburbs. 'In all things,' declared Wordsworth, 'I saw one life, and felt that it was joy.'[4] It was this possibility of a profound joy that excited me so much, this deathless spirit, which Wordsworth perceived within Nature and in which *I* could participate.

Shakespeare's *Macbeth* was another favourite at university. I particularly loved Macbeth's soliloquy towards the end of the play, delivered immediately after he heard the news of his wife's death, in which he compared life to a lousy actor hamming it up. Life, declared Macbeth:

... is a tale
Told by an idiot, full of sound and fury,
Signifying nothing.[5]

Here was Macbeth, trapped in an infinite, meaningless sameness, in which time crept with a hellish slowness, in which life seemed like nothing but the posturings of a bad actor. In the privacy of my room, particularly on bad days, I'd read this soliloquy aloud, relishing its utter world-weariness. Why did a declaration of the emptiness of existence offer such comfort?

Literature and drama excited me far more than religion at that time. Macbeth's soliloquy expressed abject despair but at least it was proclaimed in words blazing with poetic fire - which was untrue of the dreary church sermons to which I'd been subjected over the years. By the time I was a student, the religion I'd been brought up with had become redundant in terms of my quest to find true significance in life, and, by a lazy extension, I presumed that the rituals and teachings of all religions were boring and meaningless.

The 9am philosophy lectures weren't providing much of a sense of meaning either. I was too impatient, too immature, (too sleepy), to tease out any significance from those early morning sessions on Plato or John Stuart Mill. The tutorials and lectures seemed to be dealing in dry abstractions. Wasn't there a philosophy of *living*, fresh and life-enhancing, which

I could start implementing on a day-to-day basis? It seemed not. Perhaps the philosopher Thomas Hobbes came closest to the meaning of things when he asserted that life was 'nasty, brutish and short'[6] and that human beings were motivated purely by self-interest. Perhaps the best one could hope for was to participate in a reliable 'social contract' by which human beings agreed not to devour one another.

Are human beings motivated by self-interest alone? Is there a God? Is there a spirit of love or a power in Nature which we can trust and in which we can participate? Or is all such questioning just the furious, empty babblings of a bad actor? Which of these perspectives is closest to the truth of things? Are any of them close to the truth of things? Can meaning be found which is true for all beings at all times? Or, if there is meaning in life at all, is it the responsibility of every individual to discover that meaning for themselves?

I remember that one evening, after lectures, a drinking friend, losing patience with my line of conversation, wiped the foam from his upper lip and addressed me thus:

'Questions! Questions! There comes a point, Al,' he said, 'when you've got to stop asking questions and start enjoying life. You'll never find an answer ...'

When he was fifty years old, the great Russian novelist Leo Tolstoy lost his appetite for life. Despite being physically healthy, having a loving family and friends, and being widely praised and respected, Tolstoy's disenchantment with life was total. His existence suddenly seemed utterly meaningless. He felt as if some terrible cosmic joke had been played upon him, and his desire to leave life became as strong as his previous desire to live had been. It was in this state of mind that he was overwhelmed by an urgent questioning, a questioning which would not let him rest for days and nights on end...

My question - that which at the age of fifty brought me to the verge of suicide - was the simplest of questions, lying in the soul of every man from the foolish child to the wisest elder: it was a question without an answer to which one cannot live, as I had found by experience. It was: 'Why should I live, why wish for anything, or do anything?' It can also be expressed thus: 'Is there any meaning in my life that the inevitable death awaiting me does not destroy?'[7]

For me, as I left university and began to make my way in the world, the questions that were plaguing me became more insistent. In many ways I just wanted to forget about them. I wanted to enjoy my life. But with no answers to these questions, life seemed more and more meaningless.

It was in the midst of this obsessive questioning that I remembered the series of eight lectures which had been given during those early morning philosophy classes at university. The man who'd delivered these talks had only appeared for those eight weeks and he'd seemed quite unlike the rest of our lecturers. He was a lot younger, for one thing. He didn't wear a suit or a tie or a gown, and he didn't carry a briefcase. He breezed in with a rucksack on his back and a pair of mountain boots on his feet. He wore a tatty old tweed jacket. He had long hair which fell down over his shoulders, and very bright eyes which seemed unnaturally large behind a huge pair of spectacles. He brought with him, into the dusty lecture hall, a sense of the outdoors, a whiff of ozone. He had a soft voice but he spoke with a calm assurance. His subject was Buddhism.

This book is concerned with how Buddhism responds to 'the simplest of questions'. Can we discover a meaning to our lives that the prospect of death does not destroy or undo? When in the midst of my own obsessive questioning,

Questions! Questions!

I recalled those eight lectures on Buddhism, I couldn't remember the content of any of them. It was the strange lecturer I remembered. But it was that memory, amongst other things, which inspired me to explore Buddhism. Almost immediately I found that the Buddha's teaching provided answers to some of my questions. It did this by directing me to the very source of those questions, to the basic experience from which they arose... Buddhism begins with the universal experience of suffering, and it's with this theme that we begin our investigation into meaning.

1

Suffering

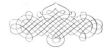

ALEXANDER SOLZHENITSYN, THE RUSSIAN WRITER, was exiled from his homeland in 1974 for making the world aware of the Gulag, the Soviet Union's forced labour camp system in which thirty million people died. In exile, as well as decrying the evils of Soviet communism, Solzhenitsyn criticized what he saw as the spiritual enfeeblement of the West. He accused the West of losing its soul, saying that Westerners had become slaves to a hedonistic lifestyle, worshipping comfort and material things. He said that human beings longed for 'things higher, warmer and purer'[8] than those offered by modern living habits. Such extreme and ultimately meaningless hedonism was a burden which needed to be shaken off to give 'free rein to the spirit that distinguishes us from the animal world'.[9]

Perhaps wise men and women down the ages have always scolded their contemporaries for prizing the sensual and material over the spiritual. Perhaps the spiritual enfeeblement decried by Solzhenitsyn isn't just a symptom of our times. The Christian mystic Dame Julian of Norwich, surveying her medieval world, declared that, 'we are seeking our rest

in trivial things - that cannot satisfy'.[10] Yet the sheer extent
of the wealth and material comfort into which most of us in
the West have been born offers temptations, challenges and
opportunities which may be unique in history.

If we're content with a hedonistic lifestyle, with the accumu-
lation of wealth and possessions, then it goes without saying
that we won't be searching for a sense of meaning in our lives.
If you're reading this book, then chances are that hedonism,
consumerism and materialism aren't enough to satisfy the deep-
est longings of your heart and that a good standard of
living is not your ultimate criterion for leading a meaningful
and happy life. But what's wrong with the enjoyment of the
senses? What's wrong with seizing the day, going clubbing,
wearing nice clothes, accessing the world wide party on the PC?
What's wrong with simply enjoying sex, food and shopping?

Nothing *per se*. Enjoyment is a human need. It's just that
hedonism as a way of life, as a touchstone for meaning, leaves
something out. That something can render such a hedonistic
lifestyle meaningless or obsolete in the time it takes for a knife
to flash, a market to fall or an artery to clog.

According to the legend of the life of the Buddha, it
was prophesied that Siddhartha (the Buddha to be) would
grow up to become either a celebrated and mighty warrior,
'trampling the neck of his enemies, a king of kings,'[11] or a
great *spiritual* conqueror, delivering men from ignorance.
Siddhartha's father, King Suddhodana, was passionate that
his son should follow their ancestors in pursuing the more
conventional path of the warrior. To this end, the king
made sure that Siddhartha was secluded from anything
which might provoke a questioning in his mind, a questioning which might deflect him from the life of a soldier. So
Siddhartha, according to the legend, was shielded from the

outside world. He pursued the traditional sports and martial exercises of his warrior clan. He lived a life of refined luxury and comfort in which he saw little of the outside world. We're told that King Suddhodana built Siddhartha three pleasure mansions, each with beautiful gardens and a pavilion dedicated to singing, dancing and delight. And a wife was found for the young prince. Yashodhara was the most radiant girl in the kingdom. Sir Edwin Arnold's poem, *The Light of Asia*, tells us that she had 'eyes like a hind's in love-time'[12] and a face so beautiful that 'words cannot paint its spell'.[13] Siddhartha fell deeply in love with her.

The king made sure that every kind of pleasure and comfort was provided for his son. Any discontent, any questioning, had to be pre-empted. Suddhodana's efforts almost beg for some kind of comic treatment. Aware, perhaps, of a restlessness in his son's nature, we can imagine the king, in his anxiety, being forced into ever more ridiculous scenarios in order to conceal the facts of life from Siddhartha: making sure that all of his grey hairs, and those of his ministers, were dyed black by the palace barber; fining all moaners and grumblers; asking persistent moaners and grumblers to find a different situation; ensuring that at the veterans' parade, the ex-servicemen who had lost limbs or were particularly physically impaired were discreetly hidden away; issuing edicts demanding a cheerful demeanour and bright robes at all times; outlawing depression; screening all the dancing girls for physical flaws; censoring the entertainment; making sure that the palace was primarily an environment for beautiful people - for the energetic, the witty, the gregarious, the pretty, the happy, the young ...

What was it that the Buddha's father was so afraid of? What was this *something* that he knew, more than anything, might deflect Siddhartha from the path of the warrior? What is it that fundamentally challenges hedonism as a meaningful way of life?

At first, Siddhartha didn't question this life of hedonism too closely, but eventually he became restless enough to wonder what life was like outside the palace walls. He decided to find out, and asked Channa, his charioteer, to drive him into the city. It was here that Siddhartha saw the four sights of legend, the sights which would change his life. We'll look at the fourth sight later. The first three sights shattered his world. The legend tells us that, on his journey, Siddhartha saw an old man, a sick man and a corpse. Presumably he knew, on some level, that all human beings were heir to decay and death. Here, in the teeming city, he suddenly realized it in the depths of his heart. The old man with toothless jaws, shaking limbs and shrivelled skin; the stricken wretch groaning, weeping and gasping for breath, his body racked with plague; the corpse carried to the cremation ground and engulfed by flames on the funeral pyre; these sights revealed the truth to Siddhartha. *This was what happened to everyone.* To himself, to all whom he loved - to everyone! What meaning could his life have now? All that enjoyment and luxury was a cruel joke in the face of what he had now seen, and Siddhartha realized it with a cry of anguish:

... The veil is rent
Which blinded me! I am as all these men
Who cry upon their gods and are not heard
Or are not heeded - yet there must be aid!
For them and me and all there must be help!
Perchance the gods have need of help themselves
Being so feeble that when sad lips cry
They cannot save! [14]

The three sights he had so far seen, which became legendary, symbolized all that his father had shielded Siddhartha from, all that the king had so feared would deflect his son from the path of lordly conquest. And, because he had shielded him from those things for so long, Suddhodana's efforts had the opposite effect from that which they were intended to produce. When Siddhartha was, finally, faced with the cruel realities of life, disenchantment came with an added, shattering force. For him it had seemed lovely to live and 'life a sunlit dream',[15] but now the veil was rent and the dream destroyed.

To experience any kind of truly meaningful life, our 'sunlit dreams' must dissolve. Much of the life around us takes place in the modern equivalent of Siddhartha's palace, with mass advertising and constant entertainment and music to perpetuate the dream. In this dream, a true awareness of suffering has little place, and when we do encounter an approximation to it, in movies or television for example, our responses are often guided towards an impotent anxiety, a sentimental pity or (very frequently) a ghoulish delight. Heirs as we are in the West to a high life-expectancy and good standards of health, suffering tends to be seen as an aberration from the norm. Death, in this dream state, is something that happens to other people. Self-help prophets sell mental hygiene like toothpaste, and stress that we *ought* to be happy, that unhappiness is a symptom of maladjustment, and that with a positive enough attitude, success and happiness, (our unalterable birthrights), are ours for the taking.

Eventually, for anyone who is the least bit sensitive, the dream does begin to dissolve and we begin to wake up to the reality of suffering. Our unhappiness demands a remedy. Someone we love dies. The suffering in the world gets through the filters of the media and our own defences. But the sight of suffering doesn't *necessarily* set us on a search for meaning. Our own pain doesn't *necessarily* ennoble us. In the face of our own and the world's suffering, we may react with quiet desperation. We may look around at the world we've been brought up in, at the conditions which we feel have given rise to our pain, at the emptiness of much of modern life, and assume that existence itself is empty and meaningless. In our shrinking world, we are all too aware of the atrocities that have been visited on our global village, and may be hard-pressed to find any meaning at all in the horror stories we've grown up with. Auschwitz, Rwanda, Bosnia, Vietnam... Such names can seem like beads on a rosary of despair.

In the face of such pain, to many of us a loving and responsible God seems a ridiculous concept. At the same time, the phrase recently splashed across British buses to advertise the joys of atheism seems feeble given the magnitude of the suffering around us. For many of us, 'There's probably no God. Now stop worrying and enjoy your life' isn't a sufficiently inspiring slogan upon which to base a meaningful life.

Yet, if we can find an appropriate response to suffering, we can begin to access a truly meaningful life. The very intensity of the pain we witness around and within us may be the impetus for us to search deeply for answers. As a young girl, the Christian mystic Julian of Norwich would have witnessed the horrors of the Black Death. The world may even have seemed to her to be coming to a catastrophic end. In later life, she could resoundingly assert her vision of eternal love in which God and man were bound, 'closer than breathing'. But to arrive at this vision, Julian must have walked a path where love was often absent. 'In order to possess what you do not possess', says T.S. Eliot in *Four Quartets*, 'You must go by the way of dispossession.' [16]

Likewise, to discover a sense of meaning in life, we may very often have to tread a path where meaning seems absent. This may be particularly true in the initial stages of our search. Yet if we can be aware of suffering, and even the feelings of meaninglessness associated with that suffering, if we can hold this tension without falling into nihilism, cynicism or despair, then our journey has truly begun. Suffering is not a virtue in itself, but an honest acknowledgement and awareness of suffering is the first step towards bringing meaning into our lives.

An acute loss of some kind, the breaking up of a romantic relationship, feelings of depression or even intense boredom... Suffering such as this, experienced on a personal level, may be what instigates our search for meaning. If, in the midst of our pain, we are able to turn away from our habitual distractions, this will give us the opportunity to examine, understand and alleviate our suffering, and to articulate what might otherwise be a vague, disempowering sense of unhappiness.

We might seize this opportunity in a number of ways: talk to a friend or friends who can help give shape to our experience, join some appropriate positive group which is committed to change, find books or music or drama which help us give voice to our suffering rather than offer a distraction from it. We may open up to pain through some creative pursuit. Channelling suffering through a poem, a painting or a song can give a pattern to that suffering, give some satisfying and meaningful form to what might otherwise remain formless and unmanageable. For many people, the initial phase of getting to grips with their own suffering comes through meeting with a therapist or counsellor.

There are many advantages to committing oneself to a course of therapy. The very act of deciding to see a counsellor is both an acknowledgement of suffering and a commitment to getting to grips with that suffering. We meet with someone who can witness our suffering without judgement. This person, in the absence, for many, of a religious context, may act as a secular priest, one of whose functions is to receive confession. We may be able to tell the counsellor or therapist things that we feel we can't tell our closest friends. If the therapist is skilful enough, they may be able to reframe some of the unhelpful stories we've been living by, or help us uncover a new story which helps us move on. We all need myths to live by and therapy may help us discover a personal myth, a story that incorporates images or characters or situations with which we particularly engage. In this way we can begin to understand and contextualize our suffering.

Of course, 'a personal myth' is really a contradiction in terms. In forging meaning in life, the articulation of such a myth is certainly a beginning, but if this personal myth is symbolized by a stream, sooner or later this stream needs to join up with a river or an ocean. Meaning must be understood in terms of a greater, deeper, more communal myth.

For, necessarily, the concentration in therapy is on ourselves. The danger is that if we continue to concentrate too much on individual self-improvement, the wider social, spiritual and mythical contexts are lost. The psychoanalyst Rollo May says that therapy has a tendency to move towards 'narcissism and excessive individualism'.[17] This tendency obstructs our access to a deeper sense of meaning in life. It's a charge repeated by the Buddhist psychoanalyst John Welwood, who says that Western psychology fails to look beyond the conventional ego or self towards a larger dimension of being. A meaningful life may begin with the acknowledgement and articulation of our own suffering, but it mustn't stop there. Eventually, we must begin to look outwards, to address the suffering in the world.

On a visit to the city of Edinburgh, the novelist Charles Dickens chanced to encounter a little boy lying quietly in an old food box which his mother had begged from a shop. The tiny, wasted child, with no recourse to medicine or nourishing food, was dying. He lay patiently and quietly, and his mother told Dickens that the boy hardly ever complained or cried. He just lay there, 'seeming to wonder what it was all about'.[18] Dickens was haunted by the look in his bright, attentive eyes, by the curious gaze with which the boy stared at this stranger to his slum dwelling, and that haunting gaze remained with the writer, demanding of him in its silence, more articulately than the words of any orator, the meaning of suffering.

Throughout his life, Dickens was always deeply aware of the pain and illness of children. His own experiences as a boy, working in a blacking factory, had made him very conscious of the vulnerable and wretched lives led by many children in similar circumstances. In his novels, and in his life, Dickens campaigned to alleviate suffering, whether it was the misery of the workhouse, the cruelty experienced in private schools or the grinding poverty of the city. In many of his novels, it is a child who symbolizes this suffering world: Oliver Twist, Jo the crossing sweeper in *Bleak House*, Little Nell in *The Old Curiosity Shop*. Often, as in the case of Jo and Little Nell, Dickens sacrifices their lives in the service of his fiction.

It's easy to be overwhelmed by the pain in the world. It's tempting to think that, individually, we can do so little that it's not worth trying to alleviate suffering. But we need not succumb to that temptation. Dickens and many of his reforming contemporaries; the previous generation of reformers who fought for the abolition of slavery; the men and women who campaign today so that others may have basic amenities like proper housing and clean water - such people have achieved results by refusing to submit to despair. Our actions, however apparently insignificant, will have consequences. In meeting suffering with compassionate action, many people find meaning in their lives, and this will be the subject of a later chapter.

Becoming aware of and trying to alleviate the suffering of others, as a way of bringing meaning into our lives, isn't straightforward. Our perspective will very much determine whether or not our response is meaningful, and there are various dangers we need to be aware of. We can, for example, respond to the suffering of others as a way of avoiding our own pain. We can become involved in a frenzy of activity by which we help others but successfully manage to distract ourselves from our own issues in the process.

Alternatively, our response to suffering may be motivated by mere pity. During a sponsored walk many years ago, I began to feel sorry for a boy with learning difficulties who seemed to be struggling, so I started to give him the occasional piggy-back. When his mother saw what I was doing, she told me in no uncertain terms that her son would walk around the course like everybody else. My sentimental response had been of no help to the boy at all.

Guilt can be another motivation to act. It could be argued that, in the end, it doesn't matter what our motivation is, as long as we alleviate suffering through giving to others. But, to bring meaning into our lives in this way, we need to feel that anything we give in response to suffering is given freely. Conscious of our own good fortune, we may, for example, respond to the picture of a sad-eyed child in the colour supplement, and to the caption underneath which reads 'Doesn't anybody *care?*' with a sizeable donation, then wonder why we feel slightly resentful and manipulated.

Guilt usually involves some fear of disapproval and this too may be an element of our response.

Such guilt and sentimental pity can subtly distance us from the suffering of another. Even Dickens occasionally fell into that trap. But, the more authentic the response to suffering, the less distance there is between the one suffering and the one responding. Dickens's boy in the food box, silently demanding of us the meaning of his pain, seems a potent symbol for the suffering world. His suffering is intense and unambiguous. We see similar sights on television, in magazines, in adverts for charities, in shop doorways. Yet to those of us who live a life free from poverty or hunger, such images might merely provoke subtle repulsion or guilt or sentimental pity. For the sight of the boy in the slum to have any deep meaning, our awareness of his suffering must resonate with an awareness of our own. We must see that ultimately, if not at this moment, we're in the same boat.

Siddhartha, the Buddha to be, witnessing the first three sights, became aware of the universality of suffering. Not just seeing, but really comprehending what he saw, old age, sickness and death didn't seem alien or other. He was forced to realise that they were not just things that would happen to 'other people'; they would happen to him too, and to everybody who he loved. This is why the sights came as such a devastating shock. Siddhartha made an imaginative connection between the old man, the sick man, the corpse, and the whole of mankind - including himself and everyone he loved. The Buddha's teaching attempts to convey the universality of suffering and, for a Buddhist, meaning in life is dependent on seeing suffering in this way.

I remember seeing a production of the Greek tragedy *Oedipus Rex* in which Oedipus discovers that he has unwittingly killed his father and married his mother. In despair, he blinds himself. When the play was over, I felt a sense of joy. I felt closer to the people around me and I had a sense that in this I wasn't alone. I noticed that people were looking at one another rather shyly, as if in recognition of something. Why did this play, with its words and images of such agony, have this effect? The production had managed to convey a sense of the universality of suffering. In communally witnessing Oedipus's dilemma, we'd seen our own suffering, our own blindness - and the blindness of humanity.

There can come a great relief when we realize that suffering isn't unique to ourselves; that we haven't been selected for victimization; that neither is this suffering merely the experience of others; that it's our human condition. Yet often we tend to look around for someone or something to blame for our own suffering and the suffering we see around us. This isn't necessarily an invalid response. Often there *is* someone or something to blame, and we need to set ourselves against injustice or intolerance or cruelty wherever we find it. But all too often, the imagined enemy is just a convenient hook on which to hang the pain of simply being human. Every day, thousands suffer or die from diseases or accidents for which nobody is, and nobody should be, accountable. We begin to answer the question of suffering when we begin to go beyond blame or accountability, when we start to see the universality of that suffering.

I recently came across a phrase in the biography of a writer who described going to visit an old friend, having been told that this friend was depressed. The writer said that he found his friend not depressed, but 'just lonely like the rest of us'. This off-hand comment had quite an effect on me, one difficult to describe. It had something to do with feeling

significantly less alone after I'd read it. As William Nicholson
has the writer C.S. Lewis declare in the play *Shadowlands*,
'We read to know we are not alone.'[19] A great book (or great
music, or great art) punctures our isolation and helps to bring
meaning into our lives. Such a book for me is J.D. Salinger's
The Catcher in the Rye. As affecting as Dickens's young
heroes and heroines are, I think that Salinger's hero speaks
more effectively to modern Westerners of our shared human
condition. I think that Holden Caulfield is less apt to invite
sentimental pity or guilt, and more likely to invite recognition. In this respect he's a more powerful symbol of suffering
for us.

The Catcher in the Rye, which was published in 1951,
describes two days in the life of 17-year-old Holden
Caulfield. At the start of the book we find out that Holden
has been expelled from school. Things go from bad to worse.
He falls out with his room-mate (who's been dating a good
friend of Holden's), and they have a fight. He leaves the
school in the middle of the night and takes a train to New
York, but doesn't want to go home and face his parents'
disappointment immediately. He checks into a cheap hotel
where he dances with some indifferent women, has a clumsy
encounter with a prostitute, and is threatened and punched
by her pimp. Through the first-person narrative we become
aware of Holden's loneliness and misery, a misery which has
probably stemmed, in part, from the death of his beloved
brother, Allie. He has a disastrous date with a girl who he's
attracted to but doesn't particularly like, gets drunk, and
goes to the pond in Central Park to try to solve the puzzle
of 'what the hell the ducks were doing'[20] during the winter.
Then he sneaks home to chat with his little sister Phoebe,
telling her he's going to leave home and live in a cabin or

a ranch. By this time it's obvious that Holden is close to a nervous collapse. He visits an old English teacher who puts him up for the night, but Holden wakes up to find the man stroking his head. Though later unsure if this was a 'perverty'[21] act or not, Holden leaves immediately and stays out in the city until morning. He meets his little sister to say goodbye but Phoebe demands to go with Holden, who tells her it's impossible. Phoebe is insistent and Holden is forced to change his mind and tell her he's going home. To mollify her, he persuades her to have a ride on the carousel at the zoo. The novel ends with Holden watching his sister ride on the carousel as the rain pours down. He feels suddenly and unaccountably happy as he watches Phoebe going round and round in her blue coat. ('God, I wish you could have been there,'[22] he tells us.)

The Catcher in the Rye is often described as a novel about adolescent alienation. It certainly is that but it's much more. It doesn't just speak for, or about, young people who can't bridge the generation gap. Neither is it just about the transition from childhood to adulthood. Holden is struggling to find any meaning in life. So many people and situations seem 'phoney' to him. ('Phoney' is his favourite word.) Holden himself, by his own admission, is a huge liar. He has a great desire, but an unfortunate inability, to communicate and connect with others. In Holden we see reflected our own isolation and loneliness, our own frustrated desire to love and be loved. Although the awkwardness and sense of alienation which Holden exemplifies is particularly strong in adolescence, his pain speaks to all ages. We sympathize with his sense of overwhelming sadness, for example, a sadness often glimpsed in small encounters in the city, as he witnesses the inner poverty of some of the lives around him.

Holden does manage to connect, to some extent, with a couple of characters - with a nun he meets in the train station and with his little sister Phoebe. More significantly, he connects with us. The book is a long conversation with the reader, and we find Holden Caulfield a hugely engaging companion. Such is the skill of the novel that the individual reader feels that he or she is the only one who can listen to or understand the boy.

The Catcher in the Rye is one of the saddest books I have ever read but it's also one of the funniest. Holden's narrative voice is hugely energetic and comic, sometimes intentionally and sometimes unintentionally so. This combination of humour and sadness often comes together to create a poignant shock of recognition. We recognize our own behaviour in Holden's. He is utterly distraught after his experience with the prostitute and her pimp, but, after being punched in the stomach, he can still imagine himself as a character in the movies, bleeding from a bullet wound to the stomach but getting his revenge on the pimp. ('The goddam movies. They can ruin you. I'm not kidding.'[23])

And what about the title? Holden has a fantasy, based on a mishearing of Robert Burns' song, 'Comin' through the rye'. He imagines himself as the guardian of thousands of children who are playing in a huge rye field at the edge of a cliff. His job is to catch the children if they start to go over the edge, to be 'a catcher in the rye'. In a way, Holden is fantasizing about doing the impossible, preserving the innocence and joy of children and protecting them from experience and suffering, from the inevitability of growing up. Yet we can't help identifying to some extent with his doomed enterprise. At a previous school, Holden had a friend who, refusing to retract a remark he made to a group of bullies, killed himself by jumping through a window. The boy had been wearing Holden's sweater at the time. Holden's desire to catch James Castle and those like him is also a mark of his sensitivity to suffering.

By the end of the novel, Holden's in a psychiatric hospital (from where he's been addressing us). It's uncertain how his life will turn out. What is certain is that his tragic, yet funny and engaging story has found a place in the Western imagination and beyond. The book has been translated into all of the world's major languages and now sells a quarter of a million copies every year with total sales of more than sixty five million. J.D. Salinger delineated a state of mind so clearly and authentically that since the book's publication, many, many people have been able to recognize in it their own sense of alienation. Realizing that the alienation they feel is not particular to them but has been experienced by another, they have been helped to overcome their feelings of isolation.

'Emotion, which is suffering, ceases to be suffering as soon as we form a clear and precise picture of it,'[24] said the philosopher Spinoza. Great art and effective religion, in forming a clear and precise picture of suffering, help us go beyond that suffering and discover meaning in life. This was, and remains, the whole purpose of the Buddha's teaching.

After his enlightenment, in his first teaching, the Buddha announced his Four Noble Truths. The first of these Truths was that the human condition was characterized by *dukkha*, or suffering. The Buddha wasn't saying that life is essentially and entirely a miserable business. (It would be impossible to square such a statement with the fact that so many ethnic Buddhists have such cheerful temperaments.) *Dukkha* incorporates the more obvious examples of suffering - physical pain, mental illness, all that we're heir to by virtue of having a human body and consciousness. But in saying that the human condition was characterized by *dukkha*, the Buddha was also pointing to an essential dissatisfaction felt by human beings, a restlessness that compels men and women to search out meaning, or, more commonly, to search out distraction.

The model of the Four Noble Truths was based on an ancient Indian medical formula: the disease, the cause of the disease, the state of health, and the regimen leading to the state of health. *Dukkha* is the disease from which humanity is suffering. The word 'disease' is a good synonym for *dukkha*. We human beings tend to suffer from a lack of ease, an anxiety. We seldom feel in harmony with the world and people around us, often experiencing a sense of disconnection or unreality or 'phoniness'. Things just don't feel right.

Dukkha is a word from the ancient Indian language Pali (in which the Buddha gave his teachings). Its roots (*dus*: bad and *kha*: space) are derived from the application of an axle to a chariot wheel and imply problems arising from a bad fit. In other words, we're driving down the motorway of life with a wobbly wheel. Most of the time we're only semi-aware of this uneasiness, this mismatch, this essential wobbliness. The Buddha challenged those who were receptive to his teaching to acknowledge their restlessness and dissatisfaction. He gave a clear and precise diagnosis of our disease as well as showing its cause and its cure, and inspiring us with a vision of supreme health.

Often we'd do anything rather than face up to the truth of this 'diagnosis'. We devise many, often ingenious, ways to avoid suffering, but such strategies usually reinforce our pain rather than alleviating it. They tend to add to our sense of meaninglessness and drive us deeper into confusion and addiction. But, as already hinted, an awareness of suffering and its universality is the first stage in bringing meaning into our lives. Suffering needn't hold us captive. It is the grit in the oyster which can produce the pearl.

Yet, for suffering to produce riches, it needs to be understood and experienced within a meaningful vision of reality. After facing up to the truth of suffering, the next stage is discovering a significant reason to live.

2

A *Why* to Live For

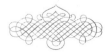

SUFFERING IS INESCAPABLE. It's the perspective we bring to bear on that suffering which determines whether we live a life of freedom or one of captivity. As Viktor Frankl put it: 'In some ways suffering ceases to be suffering at the moment it finds a meaning...' [25]

Viktor Frankl's mother, his father, his brother and his wife died in the Nazi concentration camps during the Second World War. He himself was incarcerated in Auschwitz and other camps until he was finally liberated at the end of the war, in 1945. In that same year he wrote *Man's Search for Meaning*, partly to convey his belief that life holds a potential meaning under any circumstances, even the most horrendous and miserable.

In his book, Frankl asked what freedom human beings really had, under the utterly degrading conditions of concentration camp life. Suffering from exhaustion and apathy, desensitized to the death around them, with so little value placed on their lives and with each of them becoming nothing more than a number to the majority of their captors

- what choice, asked Frankl, did he and his fellow prisoners have in the face of such circumstances? Was it possible to escape the influence of their surroundings and exert any kind of free will, let alone compassion? Were human beings formed entirely by the conditions they found themselves in and thus inevitably dehumanized by the circumstances of concentration camp life?

Frankl insisted that 'the sort of person the prisoner became was the result of inner decision, and not the result of camp influences alone', [26] that men and women might retain their human dignity even under the horrific regime of a concentration camp. He cited those who walked through the huts giving comfort to others or sacrificing their last bit of bread. He also cited the martyrs, those in the camps who bore their suffering and death with immense courage. Such people, he said, were in the minority, but everybody in the camps had had important choices and decisions to make. Those decisions perhaps seemed small and insignificant at the time, but they determined whether any given prisoner would, or would not, submit to the regime which threatened to destroy their freedom. Freedom could be fought for and retained. And that freedom was inextricably bound up with the sense of meaning and purpose in an individual's life.

Frankl's experiences in the concentration camps reinforced his belief that most modern neurosis and unhappiness didn't emerge primarily (as Freud had declared) from a frustration with one's sex life. Frankl believed that it emerged from a frustration in 'the will to meaning'. He insisted that there was nothing that helped one survive even the most terrible conditions more effectively than the belief that there was meaning in one's life. Frankl often quoted an aphorism of Nietzsche: 'He who has a *why* to live for can bear almost any *how*.' He cited the fact that those in the camps who didn't fall into despair, those who were more apt to survive, were those who had a meaningful task waiting to be fulfilled.

Those who did fall into despair, on the other hand, had no *why* to live for. They felt that life had let them down. Those who had an aim for their lives, a commitment to a future goal, found it easier to make a fundamental shift to an attitude which at least safeguarded their spiritual survival, even if their physical safety could not be assured. This shift arose from their ability to see that what was truly important was what life expected from *them*, rather than what they expected from *life*. The task that life demanded of them would differ from individual to individual. What was important was that it was a concrete task as opposed to some abstract theory, and that the task took one beyond oneself, that one's energies were 'directed to something or someone other than oneself, be it a meaning to fulfil or another human being to encounter'. [27]

Part of the task faced by Viktor Frankl and his companions in the concentration camps was the challenge of accepting the burden of their inescapable suffering with as much dignity as they could. To develop such a sense of dignity, they needed to move beyond self-pity and self-concern. It is to be hoped that we will never have to endure the kind of conditions in which Frankl found himself; there is no 'positive side' to such cruelty and inhumanity. It is simply the case that the experience of suffering, even extreme suffering, can prompt a commitment to a task which will take us beyond mere self-concern and give our lives meaning.

When he was 42, with most of his famous work (such as *Seven Samurai*) still to come, the Japanese director Kurosawa made a film which grew, he said, out of a sense of his own mortality. *Ikiru* is a film which contemplates the nature of existence and how we might find meaning in our lives, particularly in the shadow of imminent death.

Ikiru (which translates as 'To Live') tells the story of a downtrodden senior civil servant, Kanji Watanabe. At the start of the film, as the camera rests on Watanabe sitting behind his desk, a voice-over tells us that he's just killing time, that he lacks all initiative, that the town hall's red tape and meaningless intricacy has rendered him 'like a corpse' and that, basically, all he's doing is keeping his chair warm. 'Surely,' the voice suggests, 'there is no story to him.'

But there is a story to Watanabe. He is diagnosed with stomach cancer and discovers that he has only six months to live. At first, he plunges into self-pity, particularly as he's unable to share the news with anybody. He lives with his son and daughter-in-law but feels estranged from both of them. But in a city bar he opens up to a writer who takes him on a drunken tour of Tokyo's night life. There's a poignant scene in which an extremely drunk Watanabe, slumped in the corner of a bar in his crumpled overcoat and surrounded by a group of young men and women, sings an old romantic ballad in a croaking and grief-stricken voice as the tears stream down his face. It's unbearably moving and beautifully acted. The director told the actor who was playing Watanabe to 'sing the song as if you are a stranger in a world where nobody believes you exist.'[28]

Watanabe, who has hardly missed a day's work in his life, begins to absent himself from the office. He starts to spend time with Toyo, a young woman who used to work under him in his section. He takes Toyo to restaurants, buys her clothes and enjoys her happy, forthright conversation. Watanabe is hugely attracted to her vitality and youth, although that vitality exposes the aridity of his own life. At one point

Watanabe asks Toyo outright how he can become like her. He confesses to her that he longs to live as vigorously as she does, even if it's just for one day. Eventually, becoming tired of Watanabe's neediness, and concerned about how their friendship might appear to others, Toyo demands that they stop meeting. Yet his time with the girl has given Watanabe the hope that 'even I can do something'.[29]

Watanabe resolves to use his position in the town hall to push through legislation dealing with the construction of a children's playground. At the start of the film we have witnessed Watanabe ignoring the entreaties of the local mothers who are desperate to have the playground built. But now, he commits himself to the task. In a series of flashbacks (which take place after we learn of his death), we discover that Watanabe has overcome enormous obstacles and completed the construction of the playground (although others have taken the credit). We see him heroically struggling with pain and exhaustion, forcing himself to work harder and harder in order to bring the project to fruition before his death. At one point the local gangsters who wish to muscle in on the building work threaten Watanabe. 'Don't you value your life?'[30] the leader of the gangsters growls at him. Watanabe's response is to stare at the man unblinkingly, with a look of profound joy on his face, a look which renders the villain impotent. We see that Watanabe does indeed value his life, that he's discovered a *why* to live for. On the day of his death, the playground complete, we see him rocking on one of the children's swings, humming happily as the snow falls around him.

Ikiru isn't always comfortable viewing. Watanabe has found a meaning to his life but the other characters in the film, although briefly inspired by his example, soon return to their old ways and habits. At the end of the film we sympathize with one of the minor civil servants, the one character who never doubted Watanabe. Through his eyes we see how easily meaning can be taken from us, how easily our lives can be ruined by a crushing, deadening routine. And, we are challenged, as he is challenged, by the example of Watanabe's heroism.

For Watanabe, the *why* to live for was encapsulated in a commitment to a concrete task which took him beyond self-centredness. For Leo Tolstoy, who, as we've seen, experienced a profound crisis in middle age, the *why* to live for emerged slowly over a couple of years. For the great Russian novelist, the answer to the questions which had tormented him also involved going beyond self-concern. Tolstoy felt that until his crisis, he'd been living a cerebral life of convention, artificiality and personal ambition. He realized that he had to return to a simple way of life in which he could 'relieve common wants', in which the God of his childhood and of the common people might take him beyond his imprisoning and finite self and provide a sense of the infinite. Tolstoy committed himself to these tasks, devoting himself to public service, wearing simple peasant's clothing, performing manual labour and living a life of pacifism, vegetarianism and sexual abstinence. He also stopped writing the kind of novels which had brought him fame and concentrated instead on philosophical and religious works. In this way, his despair was alleviated and he felt that his life had meaning once more.

Siddhartha, the Buddha to be, was born two and a half thousand years before Leo Tolstoy*, but the questions he asked himself, as he stared into the face of suffering, were the age-old questions which Tolstoy had asked himself in the

---

* Tolstoy read and was moved by the story of Siddhartha. In his confession, he writes, 'I, like Sakya Muni, could not ride out hunting when I knew that old age, suffering and death exist. My imagination was too vivid.' [31]

depths of his despair. Was there any reason to live? Was there any purpose or meaning to life not undone and destroyed by the inevitable death which awaits all beings? The three sights, of old age, sickness and death, had turned Siddhartha's life completely upside down. And then, legend has it, he saw a fourth sight...

India has always had a tradition of wandering *sadhus*, holy men and women living without any possessions and begging for their food, people who have dropped out of society in order to understand the meaning of their existence. At the time of the Buddha, society was in particular ferment, with the old rites and customs, and the power of the priestly caste, being constantly challenged. In this time of great upheaval, new philosophical and religious ideas were being discussed and debated, and ever more people were dropping out. Perhaps the nearest contemporary comparison we can make would be with the Sixties, with all the excitement and transience of those years. We don't know what the sadhu encountered by Siddhartha believed. He was probably a dirty, wild-looking figure who wore filthy rags, purloined from a cremation ground: certainly not the kind of clothes that Siddhartha was used to and definitely not the kind of man of whom Siddhartha's father would have approved. And yet something about this dropout, who owned nothing but a begging bowl and the graveyard rags he stood up in, affected Siddhartha strongly. Perhaps it was the sadhu's calm demeanour or his sense of resolve that moved the prince. Perhaps the man seemed to know something that other people didn't. What is certain is that Siddhartha had encountered someone who had a *why* to live for.

The sight of the sadhu didn't just set Siddhartha reflecting in a rational way. It shook him to the core. For the story of the four sights to be an effective myth, we must imagine that Siddhartha was as profoundly moved by the fourth sight as he had been by the other three. Life had seemed meaningless in the face of the first three sights. The fourth sight gave Siddhartha the fervent hope that there was more to existence, a great task to which he could devote himself. Something about the sight of this ragged man, who had given up everything to search for meaning, resonated so deeply in his heart that he was inspired to follow the man's example, to commit himself to the same kind of ascetic and dedicated life. From the moment he was inspired by this wandering mendicant, although his practice would encounter many dead ends, Siddhartha's pursuit of the truth was single-minded and unshakeable. From that moment on, he had a *why* to live for.

In discovering a meaning to life, a why to live for, all the people we've met - Siddhartha, Watanabe, Tolstoy, Frankl and his companions - followed a similar trajectory. Firstly, there was an experience of suffering - an experience faced with seriousness and dignity. There was then a shift in perspective, a vision which went beyond mere self-concern. Tolstoy's vision was of a selfless, simple life in which he could relieve suffering. The wandering *sadhu* inspired Siddhartha with a vision of compassionate inquiry. Watanabe had a vision of himself as greater and kinder than he was at present. And with these visions came a task or tasks which grounded that inspiration in day-to-day reality.

The Buddhist's search for meaning in life also follows this trajectory. The vision which goes beyond self-concern is called *right view* in Buddhism, and it is the first stage of the Buddha's Noble Eightfold Path, the path which leads from suffering to liberation. Right view isn't a single event but a path in itself, a deepening alignment with the Perfect Vision which the

Buddha experienced upon his enlightenment. We'll look at the nature of this Perfect Vision again in a later chapter. For now, it's enough to say that the Buddha clearly saw that this seemingly fixed and unchanging self, which we spend our lives defending, protecting and upholding, isn't ultimately real or meaningful; that identification with this bundle of habits is, in fact, the very source of our suffering and sense of meaninglessness. Right view is a perspective on life which is a reflection (even if that reflection is faint and distant) of the vision of supreme egolessness which the Buddha experienced under the tree of enlightenment and which he attempted to articulate for the rest of his life.

The path of vision may arise in a number of ways. It may arise from meditation. It may arise from an experience of intense upset or suffering during which our old self comes apart at the seams. It may come from reading a book or seeing a painting or being in nature - some encounter through which we glimpse a deeper, more meaningful reality and are taken beyond our habitual egotism. It may arise as a mystical experience or as an actual vision.

The American writer Allen Ginsberg had such a mystical experience in 1948 when he heard the poet William Blake declaiming his poetry to him. Ginsberg said that the experience gave him a glimpse of the interconnectedness of all existence. He also said that his later experiments with drugs were partly attempts to recapture the experience. Some of Ginsberg's contemporaries, those 'angel-headed hipsters burning for the ancient heavenly connection',[32] were shattered by their drug experiences, and drug-fuelled visions produced many false prophets. But some survivors, including Ginsberg himself, managed to root their crazy wisdom, their visions of egolessness, in daily Buddhist practice and genuine altruism.

A *Why* to Live For

For some of us, more prosaically but just as authentically, the path of vision may emerge as part of our altruistic work - nursing, caring for others, looking after children... For others, right view may come from deep reflection or from the maturity which sometimes (although not inevitably) comes with old age. However it may arise, it is right view that aligns us with the Buddha's vision of reality and provides the initial impetus for Buddhist practice. Right view is a perspective on life which sees beyond egotism. A commitment to this path of vision establishes a Buddhist's *why* to live for.

But the path of vision is not enough in itself. Running simultaneously with it is the path of transformation which comprises the other seven steps of the Buddha's Noble Eightfold Path. The path of transformation provides us with concrete tasks that ground our vision in day-to-day reality. It involves every aspect of life: emotions, speech, ethics, livelihood, energy, awareness... The specific tasks involved will vary from individual to individual, and may vary in each of us from day to day. Some of us may be committed to a vocation, such as that of a doctor or a musician, a calling that seems to integrate our energies. Others may combine periods of meditation or teaching or manual work throughout the course of one day. Some of us might set ourselves the task of transforming a life of activity and doing to one of receptivity and being. Whatever the tasks we set ourselves, those tasks are illumined by our sense of perspective, of vision. And just as the tasks of transformation are given a deeper meaning by our vision, so our vision is grounded, made real in practice, and thus deepened, by the tasks we set ourselves.

The balance isn't simple to achieve. It's easy to get bogged down in day-to-day tasks and forget why we're doing them. If we have a particularly stressful job, for example, any sense of vision or perspective is in danger of becoming clouded over or temporarily lost. This is why it's so important for us to be around friends who can re-inspire us, or to go on retreat to nourish our vision.

Similarly, without the concrete tasks of transformation, we can fall into self-absorption or inertia. The mundane tasks of life can seem insignificant when we contemplate the great goal of Perfect Vision. One may have a genuine and deep concern for others, but be rendered impotent by the sheer extent of the suffering in the world. Where do we start? What can we do to make any significant change to our own habits, let alone to the state of the planet? In terms of work, it may be difficult to find a job that feels aligned with our vision. This is a real challenge for many Buddhists and may be why the Buddha devoted a whole stage of the Eightfold Path to right livelihood.

It may not be easy, but it is in the skilful performance of our regular, everyday tasks that the obstacles to freedom are removed. Small tasks done with great love and great awareness - these are the things that will eventually transform ourselves and our world. Padmasambhava, the great Buddhist master who brought Buddhism to Tibet, famously declared that, 'although my view is higher than the sky, my respect for the cause and effect of actions is as fine as grains of flour'. The profundity of his vision and his attention to the finest details of ethical action were complementary.

Dhardo Rimpoche, who died in 1990 at the age of 73, was a lama who left Tibet to become abbot of a Tibetan monastery at Bodh Gaya. He then lived for forty years in Kalimpong, where he founded an orphanage and school for Tibetan refugees and became abbot of a local monastery. In Kalimpong, he befriended Sangharakshita, my own teacher, who was motivated, partly by Dhardo Rimpoche's inspiration, eventually to return to the West and work for Buddhism.

The school which Dhardo Rimpoche founded, and through which he attempted to keep Tibetan culture alive and help the poor, was at first housed in shanties perching perilously close to the edge of a ravine. By 1977, the buildings were in such a state of disrepair, and money was so short, that Dhardo Rimpoche was forced to pawn or sell many of his possessions to tide the school over and pay the teachers' meagre salaries.

It was through meetings with Sangharakshita's western disciples that financial aid was eventually found for the school, and a handsome new building begun. Many of Sangharakshita's western disciples visited Dhardo Rimpoche and the school. Again and again, in their accounts of those visits, they testified to Rimpoche's 'profound but unostentatious kindness'. As in this account by a western visitor, Nagabodhi:

What struck me immediately was the happiness with which the kids greeted him as we passed from room to room. After all, this was the chief! Passing from one ramshackle building to another we discovered a tiny mite sobbing in an alleyway. Rimpoche left my side and gathered her in his arms, murmuring softly with real concern. Soon she was calm enough to answer his questions as he drew Tibetan characters on her little writing slate, coaxing her back to the human realm. [33]

This second account comes from another member of the Western Buddhist Order, Vijayamala, who was struck by Rimpoche's rigorous training and daily routine of intensive meditation practice and ritual:

The practices allowed him to be free - free of the tyranny of a dissipated, undisciplined mind, of what we might call the ego.

His commitment was to share that with others throughout his life. Certainly, by the time I met him, he seemed completely unpreoccupied. He was happy just to look at me and my companions for what seemed like an eternity. He was equally attentive to the young boy who was called to play to us - on a roughly strung instrument that sounded like droplets falling off Himalayan icicles in spring time - and to each of the children to whom he introduced us in our tour of the school. [34]

Dhardo Rimpoche's vision, by all accounts, was selfless and greatly compassionate. The difficulties he had to overcome in his life were many, but he never despaired. He saw it as his task to safeguard the Buddha's teaching and Tibetan culture, a great and sometimes daunting task. But, the depth of his vision and the profundity of his compassion were expressed in quiet and modest ways. He didn't seek to attract disciples. He ran a school in a series of wooden shanty huts, and taught about two hundred children. Although a very popular lama, especially latterly, he never achieved the fame of many gurus. Dhardo Rimpoche's great skill seemed to lie in fully committing himself to small tasks done with great kindness and profound attention to detail. In many respects he was an example of an ideal Buddhist.

There can be no meaning, no why to live for, without commitment. The central act of a Buddhist's life is a commitment to the Buddha, the Dharma and the Sangha: that is, to the ideal of Perfect Vision as embodied in the Buddha, to the articulation of that Perfect Vision as contained in the Buddha's teaching (the Dharma), and to the community of men and women who have, themselves, realized that Vision, or are committed to its realization (the Sangha). The act of commitment inevitably involves a closing down of options. But it's in committing ourselves to a task such as the Buddhist adventure that we go beyond superficiality, a superficiality which is experienced as a sense of meaninglessness. If we're too afraid to make mistakes, we remain on the surface of things. When we commit ourselves to a task or project that takes us beyond self-concern, we will inevitably make mistakes. A particular task may even turn out to be a dead end. But by making such a commitment we declare to ourselves and the world that we have a why to live for.

People feel that life is short. Because of this, instead of working for others, they just try to acquire wealth for themselves. If we live in this way, we become isolated. Our lives become like bubbles on the surface of water. But people can be inspired by action. If they see something is happening, they start to give … If you work hard in the right way, it will spread like light. (Dhardo Rimpoche)[35]

Such a striving for the welfare of others, a commitment to a task and vision beyond self-concern, the desire to 'relieve common wants', could be neatly encapsulated in the word 'love'. Love is such an ambiguous word, with so many complex, individual and even contradictory associations, that it's tempting to avoid bringing it into this discussion altogether. Yet, when we consult the depths of our hearts and ask ourselves the meaning of our lives, it's this single word, 'love', which so often rises to consciousness. It seems that no other word will do. Perhaps, then, it's time to ask, with Cole Porter, what is 'this funny thing called love'?

3

'Love is the Answer'

MANY YEARS AGO, when I still regularly frequented hostelries, I chanced to come across a piece of graffiti on a pub wall. 'Love is the answer,' someone had written, in bold black letters. Underneath this, somebody else had written, in equally assertive lettering, 'What's the *&£!!*$ question?' Somewhere, somehow, we know that love provides the meaning, the answer, to our lives. But - well, what is the question?

Love can mean many different things at many different times, but every kind of love is an attempt to travel beyond the imprisoning borders of the ego and make contact with the foreign country which is the other. The pursuit of romance is one such attempt. For centuries romantic love has offered us all a *why* to live for. It's a tradition which has been celebrated from the time of the troubadours, by Shakespeare, by Burns, by the billion and one popular songs on the airwaves, in lyrics of poignant tenderness or exhausting banality.

The writers of love lyrics don't go in for restraint. As far as I know, there's no love lyric which celebrates the fact that the beloved makes the lover feel fairly happy, slightly better or mildly content. Romantic love renounces the lukewarm and embraces the language of deep meaning, grand design and utter certainty. The lover tells us that the beloved 'means everything to me', 'is my destiny', 'is my A to Z', 'is my life, my love, my reason to be'. When the beloved has, understandably, had enough of such hyperbole and has departed on the next available train, the lover tells us that they are crying 'a sea of tears', that 'my life is over', that 'the sun has gone out' and that 'the stars have fallen from the sky'.

We may disagree that the object of our affections is our destiny or that they mean everything to us, but the pursuit of love (in its romantic aspect) is synonymous, for many of us, with the pursuit of meaning. The feeling of emptiness that often follows the breakup of a romantic relationship can be an indicator as to how much our sense of meaning has been tied up with that relationship.

The romantic relationship can seem a marvellous and pleasurable shortcut to meaning: to delight in another and be delighted in, to care for another and be cared for, to get such pleasure from and give such pleasure to another... For those of us who can be skilful, courageous and adaptable within such relationships, the meaning they can provide isn't to be undervalued, because if the relationship is to survive or mature, to be more than some mutual fantasy, we will be challenged to change and grow, challenged truly to empathize with another human being. This will inevitably mean going beyond our self-concern. It will also mean dealing with the insecurities, sense of threat and boundary issues thrown up by such relationships.

Sexual relationships are full of contradictions which we have to negotiate if the relationship is to remain meaningful. We have to take risks and let down barriers of mistrust and fear in order to let the other into our world. At the same time, we don't want to merge with the other and, either subtly or significantly, lose our autonomy. The other must remain special, but to what extent does this impinge on our other friendships and connections? We want to preserve the relationship but we need to risk everything at times in order not to compromise ourselves ethically. We want excitement and freedom but we also want reassurance and commitment. We have to deal with intensely felt emotions which can seem to be pulling in different directions at the same time - anger and insecurity, concern and desire... And how do we find that balance between being the controller and being the one controlled?

If we can work effectively with such contradictions, we can experience a love which is liberating and nourishing, which brings a sense of meaning to our lives. Yet such is the power of the romantic myth that there are others of us, less successful in affairs of the heart, who might be forgiven for thinking that our lives are meaningless without such a relationship. Here we are on a bleak November evening, taking our dinner-for-one from the microwave, imagining an arid life full of such evenings, without a significant other to share our bed or our ratatouille, concluding perhaps that we've fundamentally failed as human beings. At times like these, we might turn for comfort to our well-thumbed copy of *The Female Eunuch*:

Love, love, love - all the wretched cant of it, masking egotism, lust, masochism, fantasy under a mythology of sentimental postures, a welter of self-induced miseries and joys, blinding and masking the essential personalities in the frozen gestures of courtship, in the kissing and the dating and the desire, the com-pliments and the quarrels which vivify its essential barrenness. [36]

The passage reminds us of the less attractive aspects of romantic love and how easy it is to 'bind to ourselves a joy', in Blake's words. Romantic love is a power which can attenuate the ego. It can also reinforce it. Germaine Greer's cry from the heart is just as refreshing now as it was when it was written in 1970. Such an articulate rant helps liberate us from the oppressive sense that we are nothing without a romantic relationship, that Cupid has a monopoly on meaning and that there shall be no other gods before Him. Romantic love may provide some of the meaning some of the time, but it can't provide all of the meaning all of the time. Just as, to experience real meaning in our lives, we must go beyond egoistic self-concern, so too we must go beyond exclusivity. Those of us involved in any kind of mature romantic partnership or relationship wouldn't begin to pretend that such a relationship provides all of the meaning in our lives. The suffering world is too much with us, for one thing.

We've seen that our sense of meaning in life and our perspective on life are very much interlinked. The broader our perspective in terms of concern and compassion, the more meaningful our lives will be. In terms of discovering meaning in life, the romantic relationship is limited because of its exclusivity. The whole of the Buddhist life is about learning to love well and broadly, seeking to go beyond exclusivity. This doesn't mean that an aspiring Buddhist can't have favourites, particular friends or romantic relationships. But, it means that such relationships should ideally be experienced within a very expansive perspective.

The *metta bhavana* meditation practice is one way in which a Buddhist extends this perspective of concern. In the practice, we begin by generating a sense of loving-kindness towards ourselves, and then we systematically extend that love to include a good friend, a person to whom we're indifferent, somebody we dislike and, finally, all beings that we can imagine. The practice of the *metta bhavana*, or development of universal loving-kindness, challenges us to experience deeper and deeper levels of empathy. We're asked to value others as ourselves. Such a love excludes nobody. In describing the practice of universal loving-kindness, the Buddha compared it to the love of a mother for her only child. It's a paradoxical image - this profound and nurturing love, normally directed to one person, now extended to include all beings that we can conceivably imagine.

Universal loving-kindness is the ideal by which we orientate ourselves in this meditation practice. In practical terms, the *metta bhavana* demands that we descend from the heights and take what we've gained from the meditation into our everyday lives. This usually means considering the next small, kindly act. 'In this life,' said Mother Theresa, 'we cannot do great things. We can only do small things with great love.' But it is these small things done with great love which give meaning to our lives. The smallest acts of kindness tangibly make our lives more joyful and more meaningful.

Loving-kindness could be defined as going beyond our self-concern in order to sympathize with another. But to embrace this kindness fully and to trust the meaning that it can bring to our lives, we may have to address feelings of doubt or cynicism. We may subscribe to the belief (though it may only be vaguely conscious) that we're naturally self-serving and that kindness is always ultimately selfish. That is, we are only kind because it's in our interests to be so. Such a view will obviously inhibit our ability to give to others. It's a view which is gaining more and more currency. Richard Dawkins, for example, writes in *The Selfish Gene*:

Human society based simply on the gene's law of universal ruthless selfishness would be a very nasty society in which to live. But unfortunately however much we deplore something, this does not stop it being true. [37]

'Love is the Answer'

In their book *On Kindness*, Adam Philips and Barbara Taylor set about refuting such arguments. They take issue with the idea that we act utterly and fundamentally out of self-interest and that any act or feeling of empathy is rooted in basic self-preservation. They observe that there's a basic contemporary distrust of kindness but argue that the individualism that gives rise to such a view is a very recent phenomenon and would be refuted by thinkers from the Stoic philosophers to the Victorians (including Charles Darwin).

On Kindness is refreshing in its assertion that openheartedness is natural to human beings. For whatever reasons, we contemporary men and women seem to trust the evil in our natures over the good. The book asks us to place our trust in kindness, arguing that it's this which provides the true meaning to our lives and that, 'everything that is against kindness is an assault on our hope'.[38]

It is true that we have a deep-rooted tendency towards self-centredness. But such self-centredness is painful to experience and results in feelings of alienation and meaninglessness, and once we are aware of this, we are naturally going to want to overcome it. As natural as our egotism is our desire to transcend it, to find meaning in life by reaching out to others through kindness, sympathy, altruism and generosity, and experiencing the sheer fun and pleasure of giving to another. Perhaps the current cynicism about kindness is based on an assumption that a kindly act (a 'good deed') can only be performed out of tight-lipped, constipated, self-abnegating duty. It's this kind of assumption which Sangharakshita satirizes when he suggests that, rather than giving 'until it hurts', a Buddhist should 'give till you swoon with joy'. Kindness may incorporate duty but it's more than that. It's an expression of human vitality, another theme which *On Kindness* explores.

Our very exuberance and energy as human beings cannot be contained within self-concern. Kindness is an expression of our enjoyment of being alive, a joy which, ultimately, cannot be contained within the boundaries of our selves.

Nobody would argue with the fact that, at times, we can delight in the misfortunes of others. But, the Buddha recognized our great capacity for 'sympathetic joy', and stressed the importance of cultivating it. This positive quality is very highly regarded in Buddhism and is connected with *metta*, loving-kindness. When *metta* comes in contact with another's pain, the emotion that arises is compassion. When *metta* meets the happiness and well-being of another, the natural and inevitable result is a sympathetic delight.

Such a sympathetic delight in another may be experienced most fully within friendship. Our romantic relationships almost invariably take priority over our friendships, which we can rather take for granted. But, free of the neuroses that so easily creep into our love affairs, our friendships can at times generate more mutual sympathy than romantic relationships, and they are often more durable. Within a close friendship we may sense the truth that we're not merely individual splinters of selfhood; on some very basic level we're connected to one another. A friendship, in which we relate to one another on the basis of our positive qualities, can be a delightful and effective way of breaking down the barriers between self and other. In this respect, spiritual friendship has always been very much valued within Buddhism.

I imagine that throughout history Buddhists, committed to a monastic life, have delighted in one another's company. We may presume such a life to be dry and lacking passion, but the very opposite may be the case. It's impossible to sustain a spiritual life which is consistently emotionally arid. Those

Buddhists who decide on a celibate life deny themselves the intimacy, pleasure and affection which can be found in love affairs or in marriage, but passion and emotional connection can be found elsewhere - in deep meditation, for example, in Buddhist worship, and in friendship.

I recently came across a book which catalogued the rules of monastic discipline laid down for some of the early Buddhist monks. You might think that such a list would be a very dry affair, but it was fascinating to get a glimpse into the lives of those monks, who lived centuries ago and were so different from us in some respects, and yet so similar to us too. One rule forbade tickling. The rule had apparently been made because a certain monk was tickled so hard that he died. A sad little story, but I found it somehow heartening to come across this evidence that those monks were playful people who delighted in one another's company. There are certainly worse ways to go than to die laughing in the company of good (though admittedly rather careless) friends.

We have deep and abiding impulses to go beyond our self-concern. Kindness, empathy, generosity, altruism, concern, compassion, delighting in the joy and happiness of others... All these positive emotions, which could be loosely gathered under the title 'love', seek expression in our lives and help us move from isolation and alienation to meaning and connection. The more such feelings and impulses are blocked or ignored, the more we will experience our lives as meaningless. They demand an outlet.

I've experienced this most strongly, paradoxically enough, on solitary retreats. It's happened regularly. At some point, I invariably begin to wonder why I'm practising, why I'm a Buddhist. It just doesn't seem enough to practise for my own liberation or peace of mind. To make any sense out of my retreat, to make the most of the abundance of joyful energy produced by it, I eventually have to acknowledge that I'm also practising for others. Otherwise the retreat seems meaningless. Many Buddhists have talked about a similar process within their practice generally. There seems to come a point where there's a fundamental shift in perspective, an acknowledgement that one must practise Buddhism for oneself *and* others. It just seems a natural expression of our practice. We may already have understood this theoretically, but such an acknowledgement is an intuitive gut-feeling which we don't doubt to be true.

Worship and devotion are further examples of loving impulses which demand expression. To discover something, or someone, of worth and to devote ourselves to it, or them, is a natural and necessary human volition. 'We are adoring beings,'[39] says A.N. Wilson in *God's Funeral*, and the death of God, or any cynicism or repulsion we feel in relation to the words 'worship' or 'devotion', won't save us from the fact. Devotion will out. It may not always find an appropriate channel, but it can't be suppressed. With the decline of religious devotion, the cult of celebrity worship has become ever more intense. Actors, sportsmen and women, musicians, TV personalities... These are now the conventional objects of worship. It's no coincidence that they have names like Madonna and Prince, or that they live in vast estates called Neverland.† They are the new gods. Often they're quite literally worshipped to death, because, of course, they're mere mortals and are unable to bear the weight of such devotion. Diana, Princess of Wales, was just one casualty of many, and the emotion surrounding her death and

† At the time of writing, Michael Jackson had just died. The day's headline reads - 'JACKO TO LIE IN STATE IN NEVERLAND'

funeral revealed a desperate longing for a collective focus for devotion and worship.

Sangharakshita makes the point that even the Buddha, who was more highly developed than any other living being, needed a focus for his devotion. After his enlightenment, there being nobody at all from whom he could learn anything more, spiritually speaking, the Buddha resolved to worship the eternal truth that he had discovered:

This is really an astonishing episode. It shows that even a Buddha 'needs' (not that the Enlightened mind can be literally in need of anything) to honour and respect something. Even a Buddha needs to offer worship. [40]

One reason why so many people experience a sense of meaninglessness in their lives is that the channels open to them for expressing love in all its many manifestations are limited or inappropriate. In the past, love of different kinds was distributed among mentors, friends, teachers, leaders, lovers, extended family, saints, archetypes and gods. These days, within a shrinking network of relationships, we tend to seek satisfaction for all the different aspects of love from our relationships with our nearest and dearest alone. This puts a huge and inappropriate weight of expectation upon the members of our family and our romantic partners, and in our desperation to have our needs met, we can end up idealizing them, and then demonizing them in reaction. It's not surprising that romantic relationships buckle under the strain. So many popular songs express the kind of devotion which used to be called 'religious'. Can our boyfriend or girlfriend really bear the kind of homage which in the past was carried by the saints and the gods?

I was reading a couple of books in tandem recently. One was the autobiography of Edmund White, the other the autobiography of a Tibetan monk, and I was struck by the similarity in tone, vocabulary and intensity between the two. In a chapter about his teacher, the monk described an intense love for the man he called his 'master', expressing a desire to do anything for this man, who had given him so much. In similarly passionate terms, Edmund White wrote about a sexual relationship which had just ended, leaving him heartbroken. This particular chapter was called 'My Master' and concerned a relationship in which he was the 'slave' and his younger partner was the 'master'. The gratitude which was his main erotic emotion, and which he felt so intensely, shaded into an obsession which undermined his self-esteem. He didn't respect himself, he tells us. He was content instead 'to worship at this living shrine'.[41]

I don't want to appear pejorative (Edmund White's book is candid, refreshing and highly readable.) I just want to make the point that part of the process of discovering meaning in life is finding the appropriate channel for the appropriate emotion. This isn't easy, particularly when we're considering love. The words 'master', 'slave', 'mistress', 'servant', 'service', 'worship', 'devotion', 'devotee', 'teacher' are regularly typed into the search engines of Internet sex sites, but I suspect that everybody is searching for more than sex. Much more. Happy are those of us who can separate out all the different strands of love, and find appropriate channels for them all. A sense of meaning in life is greatly enhanced by the ability to distinguish and express love for friends, parents, teachers, lovers, the Buddha, and, of course, oneself.

When I first went along to a Buddhist centre and was invited to spend five minutes developing feelings of loving-kindness towards myself, it seemed like sheer self-indulgence, blasphemy even. Yet it seems obvious to me now that without a basic love for yourself, it is impossible to love others. A lack of self-worth is one of the thorniest difficulties many of us experience. As W.S. Gilbert (of Gilbert and Sullivan) put it: 'You have no idea what a poor opinion I have of myself - and how little I deserve it.'[42] A poor opinion of ourselves, based on mere conditioning and habit, needs to be jettisoned if we wish to have a meaningful life.

A few years ago I had a dream in which I was standing in a chamber, in a court of law, surrounded by benches and high, forbidding chairs. I knew that soon jurors, judges and, who knows, perhaps even an executioner, would enter. What's more, I knew that I would be dealt with harshly and that every one of those jurors and judges would have my face. I can't remember what I'd done. Perhaps I'd spread too much butter on my scone. But, I knew exactly what the verdict would be: *very, very guilty*.

One of the more humiliating realizations of my spiritual life is how harshly I can judge myself. I've discovered too, rather to my surprise, that spiritual practitioners, including many Buddhists I know, are prone to this. If we're trying to grow and develop spiritually, then we have a goal which we want to attain, and the distance between that goal and where we are now can sometimes seem very great. If we're not careful, we can berate ourselves violently for not being further on than we are, for falling into the same negative habits again, for failing to live up to our ideals. To experience such harsh self-judgement is very unpleasant. Who wants to be constantly nagged at in this way? It also tends to be counterproductive. Not receiving much kindness from ourselves, we often run into the arms of the very distractions and pleasures we're condemning ourselves for craving.

The Buddhist journey towards meaning is the journey of a lifetime (traditionally, many lifetimes). It must be travelled with patience, kindness and self-love - not self-obsession, or self-indulgence, or self-pity, but a self-love that brings a kindly awareness to all that we do and say, and is constantly forgiving of our flaws and faults. When we make mistakes, we can acknowledge these to ourselves or to our friends without judgement. We may feel justifiably ashamed if we have acted badly, but this is different from the kind of self-hatred to which many of us are so prone.

Buddhists attempt to love others as we would love ourselves. Those of us who have low self-esteem can remind ourselves that it's also important to love ourselves as we would love others. After all, we kick around with ourselves every minute of every day. We're going to spend an entire lifetime with ourselves, so it seems important that we get along. If we're practising Buddhism effectively, we'll have a growing, kindly curiosity about this strange creature, who we assume we know so well, but who is essentially as mysterious, complicated and surprising as everybody else.

For a Buddhist, love both for self and for others is illuminated by the perspective of universal loving-kindness. Ultimately, meaning for a Buddhist is fixed by this pole star. The Buddhist ideal is not just to strive for liberation for oneself alone, or to renounce self-love in order that others may benefit, or to wish for the greatest happiness for the greatest number, or to work for salvation for the believer and no one else. For a true Buddhist, no one is beyond the pale. All beings whatsoever are worthy of sympathy and love. Individual beings may condemn themselves to hellish states by their own actions, but hell is not eternal in Buddhism, and, ideally, it's the duty of a Buddhist to rescue beings from hell, whether that hell is experienced within or without.

Such universal loving-kindness finds one of its most articulate expressions in the *Bodhicaryavatara* of the eighth-century Buddhist teacher, Shantideva. The *Bodhicaryavatara* is a handbook for those who wish to become Buddhas and save all beings from suffering. It's a treasury of inspiration and exhortation, an utterly challenging and ultimately joyful expression of altruism:

I am the protector of the unprotected and the caravan-leader for travellers. I have become the boat, the causeway, and the bridge for those who long to reach the further shore.

May I be a light for those in need of light. May I be a bed for those in need of rest. May I be a servant for those in need of service, for all embodied beings. [43]

Buddhists ultimately find meaning in life through an emotional impartiality, even an emotional promiscuity, a complete lack of exclusivity, and in this respect they take their lead from the Buddha. Siddhartha, the Buddha to be, having been inspired by the sight of the wandering truth-seeker, resolved to leave home and seek the meaning of life himself. To do this, he had to turn his back on his wife and child.

I've been involved in quite a few discussions in which this action of Siddhartha's was criticized as cruel and heartless. I've also been asked if Buddhists are meant to follow his example and turn their backs on their family responsibilities. But this would be to take the story too literally. If Siddhartha hadn't left his wife and child, his life would have been meaningless. It was precisely because he loved them so much that he left them. The desire for meaning, the impulse to understand the cause of suffering, tormented him. What would have been the purpose, to Siddhartha's mind, of living, growing old and dying, and watching all whom he loved living, growing old and dying, without knowing why human beings suffered and whether there was any cure? Siddhartha loved his wife and child too much to remain in the palace. He loved suffering humanity too much. Love compelled him to leave and to seek the meaning of life.

But, even having decided to go, Siddhartha found it painfully difficult to tear himself away. Legend has it that, in torment, he circumambulated the sleeping figures of his wife and child three times before he was finally and fully resolved. We're told that he then summoned Channa, his charioteer, who drove him from the palace to the very edge of the forest. Here Channa pleaded with the prince to return, but Siddhartha's mind was made up. After embracing his master, the distraught Channa drove back alone.

Perhaps Siddhartha stood there for a while, poised at the beginning of his great adventure. He stood on the shore of that friendless emptiness, staring into the great forest which pulsated with danger and mystery, and perhaps he wondered whether truth could really be found there, within the formless, vast darkness to which love had brought him. And then, suddenly, the time for thinking and doubting was over and, without looking back, Siddhartha ran towards his future.

But why to the forest? Could he not have manifested his love for humanity by living amongst the sick, the poor, the old and the dying, in the city? Might he not have found the answer to the meaning of life in working selflessly and wholeheartedly for the welfare of others in the very midst of suffering?

It seems not. It seems that Siddhartha needed to discover something in the vast, uncharted space of the forest before he could respond meaningfully to the suffering of others.

'Love is the Answer'

He couldn't just immerse himself in compassionate activity without any pause between the old life and the new. He needed to reflect. To flower fully, to become imbued with wisdom, his love and compassion needed the openness of wild and untamed nature. He needed to consider, experiment and meditate. He needed silence and empty spaces.

Love needed space to breathe.

4

Pauses and Empty Spaces

IN AN ESSAY ENTITLED *Pauses and Empty Spaces*,
Sangharakshita writes about the importance of a sense of
spaciousness in art and in life. He cites the vast empty spaces
of sky or snow or water in the paintings of the Chinese and
Japanese landscape artists, observing that these spaces are
charged with a mysterious significance which is infused into
the solitary figure, tiny boat or single branch in the middle or
at the edge of the vast expanse of paper or silk. Similarly, he
goes on to say, it is from silence, stillness and spaciousness that
our lives derive their meaning:

*It is the pauses which make beautiful the music of our lives. It
is the empty spaces which give richness and significance to them.
And it is stillness which makes them truly useful.* [44]

A life without pauses and empty spaces is a meaningless
and chaotic life. More and more, we poor modern concussed
beings are subject to a barrage of sensory input. Some of us
may welcome this onslaught but I imagine that if you're
reading this book, you, like me, have to put in a fair amount

of effort to keep the chaos of noise and clutter and images at bay. Take my library in Norwich.

Actually, in some respects, I like the library in Norwich. It's housed in a building called The Forum, which has a handsome glass exterior overlooking a proud fifteenth-century church. One of the meanings of the Latin word forum is 'open space'. In front of the library building itself is a large open area which provides the city with a central meeting point. The Council has so far resisted plans to place permanent structures (such as a 'Norwich Eye') in the space, allowing it to remain available for temporary exhibitions and for people just to meet and chat. The open-plan interior of the building also creates a pleasurable sense of expansiveness and space. And the library, which is housed on two floors, is large and well stocked.

The trouble is that the library is not at all conducive to reading or studying. It's just too difficult to concentrate. The sounds of mobile phones and conversations go unchecked, there are three or four large screens constantly showing movies, and there's a 'Pizza Express' on the floor above the library. In a sense, the Norwich Forum is a bold initiative in support of the argument for the virtues of pauses and empty spaces, but there's a constant tension between the architect's vision and the noise and clutter of the interior which denies the character of the building. This is typical of public life at present; there is less and less quietness, stillness and spaciousness anywhere. Silence is no longer a possibility in public libraries. Television screens dominate the walls of pubs and gymnasiums. Travelling on public transport is increasingly stressful, as any of us who have attempted to defend our rights on the Quiet Coach of a train will testify. Television, with its increasing number of channels and its rolling news, seems the very antithesis of stillness. I'm of a generation old enough to remember the restful interludes which used to be broadcast in the intervals between TV programmes: images of waves breaking on a shore and a potter shaping a pot on his wheel. Not that I delighted in these images particularly - I was far too impatient for the start of 'The Flintstones'. But the potter's wheel reminds us of the steady erosion of the values of peace and quiet over the last few decades.

If we want to invest our lives with meaning, we need to find ways of bringing pauses and empty spaces into our lives, consciously and consistently. This means reducing our sensory input. Our immediate reaction to boredom, for example, is usually to seek more sensory input - music, television, conversation... But if we can learn to stop and reflect, if we can allow ourselves to experience the boredom and come out the other side, then we'll bring more and more significance into our lives. We need to reduce input in order to understand what's truly important to us and to digest and reflect on what we've already experienced. Just as we need to digest food, we need to digest the movies we watch, the books we read, the music we listen to and the conversations we have.

Subtraction. Exclusion. Reduction. Restraint. Renunciation. None of these words may seem initially attractive. They don't seem to speak of joy or exuberance or vitality. Rather, they conjure up an absence. But, it's only through renunciation and subtraction that we can understand what we truly value and love. Buddhist monks were called 'renunciants' and the Buddha himself was called 'the great renunciant'. Yet accounts of the lives of the Buddha and his disciples don't suggest that their lives were dry or joyless. The impression we get from this verse in the *Dhammapada* is quite the opposite:

Happy indeed we live, we for whom there are no possessions.
Feeders on rapture shall we be, like the gods of Brilliant Light. [45]

Renunciation cuts away the detritus and dead wood of our
lives so that we can discover the meaning and beauty which
exist beneath. Such beauty is very evident in the Zen poetry of
Ryokan, the Japanese hermit monk. In his mountain hermit-
age, Ryokan lived with hardly any possessions, meditated,
mended his robe, observed the changing seasons and wrote
poetry. Like Chinese and Japanese landscape paintings,
Ryokan's poems are suffused with a vast sense of spaciousness
in which we see the hermit and his few possessions with a
wonderful and touching clarity:

My hut lies in the middle of a dense forest;
Every year the green ivy grows longer.
No news of the affairs of men,
Only the occasional song of a woodcutter.
The sun shines and I mend my robe;
When the moon comes out I read Buddhist poems.
I have nothing to report, my friends.
If you want to find the meaning, stop chasing after
So many things. [45]

It's not easy for us to stop chasing after so many things.
We human beings far prefer proliferation to renunciation.
We naturally revel in proliferating. I had a friend whose
room was like a black hole. Everything disappeared into
it. I remember plucking up courage and going in there one
afternoon because all our community mugs had vanished. It
was a frightening sight. Most of the mugs were in there, as
well as a colourful variety of rogue socks, a few half-finished
meals, cascades of CDs and much else besides. But, my friend
had cleared a small space in the middle of the room and had
rather poignantly placed there, like some charm to ward off

evil, a book entitled *The Japanese Art of Feng Shui*.

It's in writing that I particularly see my own tendency to proliferation. Everything I do tends to be over-written, and at some point there comes the painful task of subtraction and editing down. Yet, it's in this process of subtraction that I begin to understand more clearly what I'm really trying to say.

Our thoughts certainly proliferate. Our minds have a huge tendency to multiply thought upon thought. Unfortunately, our education is terribly lacking in any kind of effective response. I went through school and university without a single class in which it was suggested how I might organise my thoughts, without any wise being arguing for the vital need for pauses and empty spaces. By my early twenties I was head-crammed, word-sick. My thinking had become almost pathological. Yet such obsessive thinking is pretty much the norm. Our minds, most of the time, are gridlocked, utterly choked with thoughts.

Obsessive thinking isn't just a modern problem. One of the greatest works of English literature, Shakespeare's *Hamlet*, is about a man, (a student, interestingly enough), who is unable to commit himself to a course of action. His life seems to him absurd, meaningless. He knows that he must revenge the death of his father by killing his uncle (who murdered Hamlet's father and usurped the throne), but he can't bring himself to do it. This doesn't seem to be ethical squeamishness on Hamlet's part. He just can't commit himself to action, and although the reasons for his inertia are various and complex, and have (ironically) produced a massive proliferation of critical volumes on the subject, one of the main reasons for Hamlet's inaction is that he thinks too much or, in his own words, thinks 'too precisely on th'event'.[47] For every thought, whether that thought be about suicide or murder or duty, Hamlet has a counter-thought. To be or not to be? To act or not to act? He can't decide. His dilemma pushes him into insanity. (Or is he pretending to be mad? And does he know one way or the other?)

Hamlet knows there's something corrupt and dislocated in the state and feels that it's his duty to put it right. He is nauseated by 'words, words, words' - the insincere speechifying of his murderous uncle, the tedious aphorisms of the windbag courtier Polonius, the false flattery of his old friends, Rosencrantz and Guildenstern... Yet he feels there's something dislocated in his own mind too, something which shuts him off from joy and meaning - and commitment. His 'native hue of resolution/ Is sicklied o'er with the pale cast of thought'.[48] He is imprisoned by words. By thoughts.

Hamlet does kill his uncle in the end, but not before murdering the wrong man, sending his girlfriend, Ophelia, insane, and bringing destruction upon himself, his mother and Ophelia's brother. The play wouldn't be such a tragedy if we didn't have a sense of Hamlet's greatness, of a vast, squandered potential. Which, we feel, is our potential too. It's no coincidence that Shakespeare's tragedy is one of the most loved and valued works of Western literature and that so much attention has been paid to it. Hamlet's dilemma is our dilemma. His inability to act or commit himself is our inability, and his 'thinking too precisely on th'event' is very much part of our human condition. The human tendency towards this kind of thinking goes as deep as our tendencies to hatred and neurotic desire. The Buddha knew that this conceptual proliferation (*papanca* in Pali), was at the heart of human suffering. He knew, too, that uprooting it was synonymous with freedom:

Who neither transgresses or lags behind, who has transcended all this conceptual proliferation; that monk quits bounds both here and hereafter even as the snake its worn-out skin. [49]

This all-too-human tendency to conceptual proliferation involves us in regrets about the past and anxieties about the future, in a maelstrom of thinking which prevents us from experiencing the here and now and which results in feelings of superficiality, unreality and meaninglessness. So how do we deal with *papanca*? Again, we can come back to pauses and empty spaces. We can start by simply noticing the space around things. Ajahn Sumedho says in his pamphlet, *Noticing Space*:

The space in a room is peaceful. The objects in the room can excite, repel or attract, but the space itself has no quality that excites, repels or attracts. But even though the space does not attract our attention, we can be fully aware of it when we are no longer absorbing into the objects in the room. When we reflect on the space in the room, we feel a sense of calm, because all space is the same; the space around you and the space around me is no different. [50]

Similarly, we can begin to notice the space in our minds. Our minds may seem to be full of thoughts but we can become more aware of the space around thoughts, in the same way that we can become aware of the space around objects, and thus we become less and less caught up with our habitual thought processes. It's rather like the traditional way of guarding against losing one's temper: 'Count to ten!' Simply by counting to ten, we can cease to identify with the thoughts filling our minds. Instead, we identify with the space in our minds, which immediately gives us a different perspective on things. By identifying with the space around thoughts, we bring a truer, more meaningful perspective to bear on our lives.

Pauses and Empty Spaces

For a Buddhist, periods of reflection are another way to counteract the tendency to obsessive thinking as well as the tendency to live a cluttered, unaware existence. There are many different ways to reflect. You could just sit in an armchair and observe the flow of your mind, allowing things to arrange themselves or fall into place. You could reflect in a more directed way, by dropping a question or a verse of wisdom into your mind and noticing the effect. You may like to keep a diary or a journal. Sometimes it's useful to make no effort at all. While simply going for an undistracted walk in the park, the answer to some question might just appear. But, however we do it, such reflection is absolutely essential. 'An unexamined life is not worth living,'[51] said Socrates. Reflecting on our experience inevitably results in a more meaningful life. Such reflection is very different from self-obsession which involves the kind of circular, useless thinking we've been talking about.

It's not that thinking is ineffective or harmful in itself. Reflection and clear thinking obviously go hand in hand. Indeed, clear thinking is an indispensable part of the Buddhist path. It's just that most of the thinking we do is unfocussed, habitual, unnecessary and imprisoning. One way of making our thinking more focussed is to plan in time for it, in the same way that we might plan in time for a movie or a swim. Whether we wish to think or reflect in a linear way, in an associative way, or in a way that avoids words altogether, being clear about the *purpose* of any period of thinking and reflection is also extremely useful. Another very effective way to think or reflect is with a friend or friends. This might seem paradoxical, and not very much to do with pauses and empty spaces, but such collaborative reflection can keep one's mind on track, challenge habitual woolly views, and steer one away from proliferative, obsessive and habitual tendencies of thought.

Another way of introducing stillness and spaciousness into our lives is to use the gaps between activities to bring ourselves into the present moment. We normally experience time spent queuing at the bus stop, wandering through the supermarket or waiting for the computer to fire up as 'dead time', to be endured until the business of living resumes. But, these so-called boring moments can become opportunities for awareness. During a day retreat at the Norwich Buddhist Centre, I asked everyone to spend a couple of hours wandering the city, perhaps going into the shops we usually went into, or attaching ourselves to the queues we usually attached ourselves to. But, on this occasion there would be nothing to buy and nowhere to get to. The only agenda would be to notice what was going on around us, and what was happening in our minds.

I found the longest queue in my least favourite supermarket and joined it. When I allowed my habitual impatience and irritation to fall away, I began to enjoy the process of being in this familiar environment without the familiar volition to get out and get on with my life. I began to experience a palpable sense of spaciousness and to enjoy the smells and sounds and sights around me.

In the attempt to bring space, silence and reflection into life, many Buddhists go on solitary retreats. When I first started doing this, a frequently asked question was, 'Won't it send you crazy?' - which reveals the fear we have of being alone, particularly of being alone with our own minds, without our usual distractions. It's certainly true that painful states of mind may arise on solitary retreat. With much less to distract us, we may be forced to face the more unpleasant aspects of our mind and character. But, we may also experience deeper feelings of joy and pleasure than we normally do.

I've experienced some of the happiest and some of the most painful moments in my life on solitary retreats. I've also noticed that the more joyful moments often arise as a result of staying with and experiencing the more painful emotions. I particularly remember evenings spent during a long solitary retreat in a cottage in North Uist in the middle of winter. After dinner I would stack up my peat fire and just sit looking at the flames. The desire, after a while, to read or switch on the telly (which I'd wisely concealed, like a budgie in its cage, under a cloth) was often intense. But if I just sat there, through my acute boredom, I eventually experienced prolonged periods of intense happiness. During those times I found that I could think so clearly that the concepts and words I brought to mind seemed to shine with a kind of glorious, wintry brightness.

Solitude can give us the chance to experience ourselves in our heights and in our depths. It can also help us to discover a more meaningful way of living. We may be surprised at the pleasure we experience at this opportunity to get to know ourselves better. 'I never found the companion that was so companionable as solitude,'[52] said the American writer, Henry David Thoreau.

Between 1845 and 1847, Thoreau spent twenty-six months in solitude in a cabin near Walden Pond in New England. In this experiment in living, he wanted to find out what was necessary in life and what was superfluous. He stripped his life down to the very essentials, growing his own food, patching his clothes, and trying to seclude himself from the industrialized world rapidly growing up around him.‡ He wrote about his experiences in *Walden: or Life in the Woods*, which combines both a spiritual and a very practical vision for living.

Walden Pond was rumoured to be of infinite depth and Thoreau was so intrigued by the question of how deep the pond was that he devised a new method of plumbing depths to measure it himself, finding it to be no more than a hundred feet deep. He wondered why people had insisted that the pond was bottomless and came up with a spiritual explanation: human beings need to believe in the infinite. Thoreau's attempts at a more spacious and spiritual life came to be symbolized by this stretch of water, 'looking into which the beholder measures the depth of his own nature'.[53]

Buddhists have experimented with solitary or collective adventures in alternative living for centuries. Some Buddhists choose to live in such a way all the time. For others of us, a collective or solitary retreat provides a brief but essential break from our urban environment. Living in a more natural environment gives us readier access to a sense of spaciousness than city life usually does, and provides us with natural symbols such as sea, sky or forest, through which we can see into the depths of our own natures. When we contemplate a clear blue sky, for example, and allow ourselves to be moved by its vastness and mystery, we're also glimpsing our own inner, primordial nature, unblemished by obsessive thought.

Yet, we don't always welcome such a sense of spaciousness into our lives. We may crave it, yet we fear it too, because it undermines our fixed, habitual reference points. Why else, on a solitary retreat, might we find ourselves discovering all kinds of new and cunning distractions? We feel far more comfortable

‡ It must be said that occasionally Thoreau met with friends at the weekend and took his washing back to his Mother.

identifying with *papanca*, with the endless proliferation of thoughts in our mind, than we do with the space around those thoughts. Yet the more we introduce spaciousness into our lives, the more we *identify* with and trust that space, the more meaningful our lives will become. On a solitary retreat we can let go of our tight grip on *papanca*, notice how we identify with the passing clouds of anxiety or depression or envy, and how that identification can feed into a sense of meaninglessness. We can more easily identify with the sky-like nature of our mind, with all the significance that may bring.

In one of his most famous poems, the Orkney poet George Mackay Brown uses an unusual phrase to describe the true calling of the poet: 'the interrogation of silence'.[54] It's a phrase which shouldn't really work - but it does. 'Interrogation' seems such a harsh word, a strange choice to associate with poetry or silence. But the juxtaposition of 'interrogation' and 'silence' has a strange, unsettling effect, creating an almost comical short circuit which brilliantly conveys the task of the poet. To me, the phrase also conveys the calling of a Buddhist - or of anyone who is searching for meaning in life. It conjures up the single-mindedness, concentration and spaciousness necessary to bring a sense of significance into one's life. It's also an appropriate metaphor for meditation.

Buddhist meditation involves far more than bringing pauses and empty spaces into life, but all the themes we've been exploring in this chapter - spaciousness, stillness, reflection, clear thought, silence - have a bearing on meditation practice. Essentially, Buddhist meditation has two elements - a calming aspect in which we try to cease identifying with the papanca which has hitherto driven our life, and a wisdom element, one aspect of which involves consciously considering the meaning of life.

It was to meditation that Siddhartha turned when all else had failed. After going forth into the forest, he single-mindedly committed himself to one spiritual practice after another in an attempt to discover the truth. He mastered all that the teachers he encountered had to offer, but he still wasn't satisfied. He then undertook a variety of rigorously severe ascetic practices, but, at the end of six years of striving, he felt that he was no further forward in his search. He had wholeheartedly devoted himself to practices which had seemed to offer the promise of liberation, but those practices had failed and now, exhausted and close to death, his quest for meaning in life seemed to have come to a dead end.

It was then that he remembered something that happened in his childhood. One day he had gone with his father, the king, to the countryside, for the ritual inauguration of the first ploughing of the spring. As the young Siddhartha sat under the shade of a rose apple tree watching the ploughing, his senses slowly withdrew from the scene being played out before him and he started to become absorbed in his inner experience. Time stood still, and such was the boy's sense of bliss, concentration and spaciousness that when it was time to go home, it felt to him as if no time had passed at all.

Remembering this incident many years later, Siddhartha intuitively sensed that this was the way to liberation. He sought out a shady tree by a river and sat beneath it. With a renewal of strength, having eaten a proper meal after months of starvation, he vowed that he wouldn't leave the spot until he had discovered the meaning he'd been searching for. 'Flesh may wither away,' he declared, 'blood may dry up, but until I gain enlightenment, I shall not move from this seat.' [55]

And so Siddhartha sat in meditation under the towering tree and slowly began to experience ever deeper states of blissful, spacious awareness, an awareness which transcended all boundaries of subject and object and which was thus infinite and unblemished, an awareness entirely free of *papanca*, delusion, hatred and craving. With this awareness came an overflowing of great compassion, and reflections and visions of the true nature of existence. Finally, towards the end of the night of the full moon of May (the Indian month called Wesak), just as dawn was breaking, full understanding came to the man who was now the Buddha, the Awakened One.

How do we attempt to describe this mysterious enlightenment of the Buddha, in which he finally discovered true meaning? In his epic poem *The Light of Asia,* Sir Edwin Arnold skilfully manages to describe the Buddha's enlightenment in poetic terms, using the imagery of the dawn:

...Over the spangled grass
Swept the swift footsteps of the lovely Light,
Turning the tears of Night to joyous gems,
Decking earth with radiance, 'broidering
The sinking storm-clouds with a golden fringe... [56]

Just as Walden Pond was seen by Thoreau as a symbol for the infinite, so in Arnold's poem, the Wesak dawn becomes a symbol for the Buddha's illumination of mind, for the meaning he has discovered. More than that, the dawn symbolizes the glorious potential which has suddenly been revealed for all mankind.

There is something in all of us which yearns to go beyond the finite, beyond all boundaries and limitations. We yearn for such a state but we're also terrified of it, because it threatens our dissolution. This leads us on to our next theme which, presented baldly, may seem unattractive, abstract, even repellent. Yet, in truth, it points to unbounded possibilities, to the great potential within all human beings. The theme is emptiness.

5

Emptiness

IN GLASGOW, WHERE I WAS BROUGHT UP, there are two main football teams: Glasgow Rangers, whose strip is blue and whose players were traditionally from the Protestant faith; and Glasgow Celtic, who wear green jerseys and whose players used to be exclusively Catholic. Happily, strict sectarianism is no longer enforced and the management of both teams have signed up those of the opposite faith for quite some years now. But when I was younger, religious prejudice in the city ran very deep. My father told me of a builder, a fanatical Rangers supporter, who had turned down a job because he refused to walk on green carpets. Or was it a Celtic supporter who refused to walk on blue carpets? I can't quite remember the details now, although I've never doubted the story. I *do* remember, very clearly, the ugly scenes on a bus after an 'Old Firm', Celtic versus Rangers match, and the hatred etched on the faces of the men and boys on both sides.

Such a rigid identification with a particular religion or football team (or country or family or skin colour) can seem to give life a meaning of sorts. But it's a meaning which is based on violent division, a meaning which must always perceive an enemy. Such bigoted views divide communities, and they also divide the mind. As sources of meaning, they're useless.

Our sense of meaning is inextricably bound up with our beliefs and views, with our perspective on life. These views, beliefs and perspectives affect everything we do: what we eat, what we wear, how we look at colour, what carpets we choose to walk on, how we behave towards others, how we see objects. For a vegetarian and a farmer, for example, a cow will have a different meaning. For the artist and the forester the same tree will, again, mean something quite different.

The perspective and beliefs we bring to bear on ourselves profoundly affect us too. Many things determine how we see ourselves: our education, our parents, our religion or lack of religion, the books we read, the movies we watch, the music we listen to... The list is endless. A good teacher, for example, can profoundly influence how we look at ourselves. He or she might see some talent or potential in us, draw that potential out, and give us the confidence to perceive it for ourselves. The self-belief that such teachers can instil can't be overestimated. Time after time we hear an artist or a singer or a spiritual practitioner movingly describe a teacher or mentor who has given them a sense of inspiration and meaning simply by believing in them. Similarly, a bad teacher can destroy our self-confidence. In the presence of a cruel or foolish teacher, we can experience ourselves as insignificant, and even feel physically smaller.

Our minds are a soup of views and beliefs: romantic, divisive, inclusive, nihilistic, sentimental, eternalist, spiritual, political, cynical - all contributing to a sense of meaning or meaninglessness, all having a bearing on how we see this self of ours. We may discover some view of life, some *ism*, to which we're particularly attracted, or with which we particularly identify, and this will obviously have a powerful effect upon how we see ourselves and upon our sense of meaning in life. I once read an affecting account of a college student of literature, who had committed suicide. His parents asserted that a lot of the books he'd been reading had contributed to his sense of despair, and they criticized the college authorities for providing a reading list with a great over-emphasis on nihilistic and despairing material. In this extreme case, the boy's parents believed that the views to which their son had been subjected, and with which he had closely identified, had significantly contributed to his self-destruction.

How should we approach this self of ours, to provide it with the meaning for which it longs? Should we pamper it? Challenge it? Leave it alone and hope things work out for it? Should we be kind to it? Strict with it? What does it need? Who should it trust? There are plenty of people eager to provide answers. There is, for example, a genre of writing which offers a particular perspective on the self. I jotted down a few titles from the self-help section of my local bookshop: *I Can Make You Rich; Instant Confidence; Self Matters; Change Your Life In Seven Days; Feel Happy Now; Your Best Life NOW; Life's Too F***ing Short: A Guide To Getting What YOU Want Out Of LIFE; Ten Days To Great Self-Esteem*. In this kind of literature, the self is regarded almost like the chief executive of a corporation who must construct a business plan, complete with charts and graphs and targets, in order to access the guaranteed (and almost instant) riches, confidence and success which provide meaning in life.

It's the immediacy of the solution that's a bit suspect. One can't help being reminded of those old Westerns where Doctor Quack, in dusty black suit and top hat, peddles his bottles of patent cure-alls from the back of a covered wagon.

All religions have grappled with the question of how to view the self. The traditional Christian doctrine of original sin, for example, has provided a perspective on the self which has profoundly affected millions of people over the centuries. A myth to describe our human alienation, its literal application has had the unfortunate effect that countless human beings have experienced an essential distrust of themselves. It's a distrust which still hangs around today, even in the psyches of non-believers, and contributes to the sense of depression, meaninglessness and low self-esteem which so many people feel.

How to view the self was a dilemma for Siddhartha. He was determined to discover the meaning of life, but what perspective on body and mind might give him access to that meaning? Self-indulgence was out of the question. His hedonistic lifestyle had been exposed as meaningless by the sights of old age, sickness and death... Siddhartha decided to go to the other extreme. If he mortified the flesh, in the manner of many of the spiritual seekers of his day, might this free the soul? Through the denial of the body, might his mind become liberated and might he thereby discover true meaning?

With this hope, as we saw in the last chapter, Siddhartha strictly adhered to a regime of severe asceticism for six years. Nobody, it was said, could outdo him in the extremity of the austerities he practised. He starved himself, tortured his body and sat for hours under the ferocious Indian sun. He continued to perform all kinds of perverse ascetic practices until, on the brink of death, he realized that it just wasn't working. All his austerities had got him nowhere, and he abandoned such self-mortification totally and immediately. In doing so, he cleared the way for his final breakthrough under the bodhi tree, the tree of enlightenment.

It's difficult to engage imaginatively with the extreme nature of Siddhartha's asceticism. It is easier for us to relate to his hedonistic life in the palace, because our experience is far more like that. But we can still take a couple of useful things from this episode. Firstly, Siddhartha was willing to give up a view (in this case the view that self-mortification might provide an answer to the question of existence) when he saw that it wasn't bringing him any closer to a true sense of meaning. So often our views and our selves become enmeshed. When we identify closely with a particular view or perspective, the self can feel superficially secure in that view, even if it's a wrong view. Siddhartha was willing to admit he'd made a mistake, and to renounce the approach to life he'd been taking for years as soon as he realized it was redundant.

The other thing we can take from this story is that the way to meaning is not to set the body against the mind. The Buddha was clear on this point. Neither self-indulgence on the one hand, nor self-mortification and self-harm on the other, constitute the way forward. What then was the Buddha's perspective on the self? And, what bearing does this perspective have on the search for meaning?

The Buddha declared that our existence was characterized by three marks. One of these, *dukkha* or *suffering*, we've already looked at. He also declared that existence was characterized by *impermanence*. From planets, solar systems and galaxies down to atoms, particles and sub-particles, transience and change hold sway. And, of course, such change also governs ourselves. Our bodies are constantly changing, cells dying and being renewed, nails growing, hair thinning... But we resist perceiving the truth of impermanence in our bodies, and naturally shy away from the inevitable conclusion that the body will one day cease functioning altogether. It's easier to observe impermanence within our minds. Two minutes of honest reflection will reveal that our minds are a constant stream of thoughts, a perpetual activity of flux and flow.

The Buddha also saw, probing into the truth of impermanence even more deeply, that there is no *thing* which changes. If all 'things' are, in reality, process, then we can't abstract any thing from the process of change itself. What we call a table or a car or a bush or the self is an attempt to freeze process. It's a photograph, a label, with which we attempt to categorize, understand and deal with the dynamic nature of reality. Necessarily, to understand our world, to get through the day, we give names and labels to particular parts of the process of change and ever-shifting conditions that we experience around and within us. Once a part of the process has been named and labelled, it apparently becomes fixed and permanent; but, in truth, it's insubstantial. According to the Buddha, this *insubstantiality* was another of the marks which characterized conditioned existence.

To say that things are insubstantial is to say that any 'thing' can be most meaningfully viewed in terms of its parts and conditions. A car, for example, can't be separated from its parts - engine, headlights, seats, hub-caps, wheels and so on - and these, in turn, can't be separated from *their* constituent parts. More than that, a car is also the totality of its conditions. It cannot be said to exist separately from the man or woman who drives it, or the company who designed it, or the road networks, or the invention of the internal combustion engine. It's the same with us. We are our constituent parts - blood, skin, bone, nerves, organs, teeth... We are a flow of psychic and physical events. And we are dependent upon, and brought into being through, a vast network of conditions. As we delve into these conditions, who 'we' are becomes increasingly mysterious, increasingly insubstantial.

Take the writer of this book, sitting at his computer screen, selecting from the mind-flow words and ideas and images by which he hopes to connect with you, the reader. He could be described, in brief, as white, middle-aged, gay, middle-class, male, Buddhist, Scottish and tall. Slightly anxious, a bit impractical, quiet, intelligent, and of a creative disposition. And there you have him, suitably pigeonholed. But let us regard this interesting creature in a bit more depth.

He is the product of millions of years of evolution. He is reliant for his existence on the presence of water and an atmosphere containing some, but not too much, oxygen. He's also reliant on the maintenance of external temperatures within a limited range, a magnetic shield to block the most aggressive radiation, and food sources which supply his body with carbohydrates, protein and minerals.

He is the plans and dreams of his mother, Beatrice and his father, Ian, and he has come into being through the attraction they first felt for one another at the Tudor Ballroom in Glasgow in 1949. He has many of their attributes. (Once he became adult, he was constantly mistaken for his father on the phone.) He is partly the product of a culture and mindset which came into being after World War Two. This provided him with books, music and drama which challenged many of the values of the generations which came before him. He has been conditioned hugely by the fear which was brought about by the Cold War. He was brought up in the Church of Scotland, which instilled both a certain positive ethical sense and a sense of repression and guilt. This latter has given him a mild distrust of sensual pleasure, although the liberalization of the laws on homosexuality has provided him with a freedom unknown to previous generations. He has the slightly split personality of the Scot, that curious combination of dourness and rebellious joy. A certain degree of confidence and happiness has been brought about, in great part, by the love and companionship of parents, brother, relatives and friends. His anxiety is partly inherited from his mother, who largely inherited it from *her* parents, whose traumatic experiences during the First World War were a major contributory factor to their own insecurity and fear. His impracticality comes partly from his father, who was impractical because *his* father was wounded in the First World War and couldn't pass on any practical skills to his son. To some extent then, he has been shaped by a worldwide conflict that concluded in 1918. In his early twenties, he came in contact with a religion which was founded two and a half thousand years before his birth. He discovered that Buddhism, as taught by Sangharakshita and his disciples in the Western Buddhist Order, effectively addressed his anxiety and sense of meaninglessness.

His mind is a constant flow of thoughts. His emotions change from minute to minute, like infinitely turbulent weather patterns. For the past twenty-five years he has used meditation to bring some perspective to the essentially dynamic nature of these thoughts and emotions. Some of these he particularly identifies with. Others seem strange or alien, nothing to do with him. He is constantly intrigued by the question of what, or who, it was that made the meaningful and significant choices in his life.

The more we look at ourselves, the more we begin to discover a vast and dynamic dance of change and conditions. Such a prospect is truly threatening to our small and frightened selves, dependent as we are for our sense of security upon experiencing a sense of fixity and *permanence*. Wanting to feel in control, to assuage our insecurity we select passing emotions from the mind flow and identify with them. We identify with the conditions nearest at hand - religion, football team, family or country - and attach ourselves to them like limpets to a rock. Through habit and repetition we try to engender a sense of permanence and stability in what is, in reality, a sea of change and conditions. We attach ourselves to that which gives us pleasure and stability, and push away what we find painful or threatening.

But, what the self gains in apparent security and stability, it loses in meaning and authenticity. To bring more meaning into our lives we need to recognize and work with our deep-rooted tendencies to cling, to attach, to over-identify, to conform to rigid habit, to defend, aggressively, the boundaries of our fixed selves. In other words, as we've seen in previous chapters, we need to go beyond self-concern. The *metta bhavana* meditation practice (described in chapter 3), for example, challenges us to let go of over-identification with religion, football team, family, country, or any other group or tribe. Doing the *metta bhavana* meditation can help us understand that others feel as we do. It can help us realize that essentially we're all in the same boat, struggling with our attachments and habits and insecurities, protecting these small selves which so tenaciously cling to the familiar and comfortable, and which reject the unfamiliar and threatening. The more we can empathize with others, the more we can let go of rigid attachments and lessen our tight grip on unhelpful habits, the more we'll go beyond self-concern, and the greater sense of meaning we'll experience.

The Buddha's teaching offers a radical perspective on the self and self-transformation. It states that ultimate meaning is found in going beyond the ego entirely. Wherever there is an 'I', according to Buddhism, wherever there lurks even the subtlest sense of separate selfhood, there lurk, also, the seeds of greed and hatred. Even an over-identification with compassionate activity, with meditation, or with ritual, is a source of subtle pride and, as such, an obstacle to progress. Buddhist practice is radical to the extent that the practitioner attempts to become aware of every tiny splinter, every subtle nuance, of separate selfhood. All religious teachings attempt to direct their adherents beyond self-concern and describe practices by means of which this can be achieved. These practices provide a vision by which the practitioner can recognize and transform self-centredness, anger, materialism, the desire for power, and so on. But to few of these religious teachings (to quote Sangharakshita), 'is given the piercing eagle vision which can discern the egoism lurking in the desire for eternal life, or in the longing for communion with some personal god'. [57]

In truth, there is no fixed self, merely an ever-changing network of conditions. To embrace such a dynamic reality, fully, requires total egolessness, but such supreme egolessness, although it is to be cherished as an inspiration, is very much an ideal, a goal, rather than something we should expect ourselves to manage all at once. We work towards that goal, compassionately and patiently, with our fearful and insecure selves.

Although insubstantiality is often referred to as the characteristic of 'no-self', this phrase is ripe for misinterpretation and can lead to the belief that the self must be destroyed or annihilated. (*Nirvana*, the goal of the Buddhist life, has sometimes been translated as 'self-annihilation'.) This can give a very unappealing and misleading picture of the Buddha's teaching and can confirm critics in their belief that Buddhism is a nihilistic and life-denying religion. It's certainly true to say that a Buddhist is attempting to go, gradually, beyond the ego. But, this can't be done in an aggressive or a sudden way. This self of ours has been formed over many, many years (many, many lifetimes, according to Buddhist teaching). As Buddhists, we're not trying to annihilate ourselves. Better to say that we are, over a long duration, kindly and gently letting go of unhelpful habits, preferences and identifications, into a more adventurous and dynamic state of being. The characteristic of insubstantiality provides us with an exciting perspective. It tells us that this seemingly fixed and unchanging self can slowly be transformed, that there are visions of meaning and ways of experiencing ourselves that, to quote Sangharakshita again, 'we can grow towards in a way that is inconceivable to our present state of individuality'.[58]

Such an exciting prospect is dependent on our becoming, over the years, more and more comfortable with, and accustomed to, seeing the impermanent and non-static nature of what we call the self; seeing the insubstantiality of existence; gradually allowing the rigid boundaries of self and other, self and world, to melt away and beginning to perceive existence with the eye of egolessness. The eye of egolessness sees the deep connections between all sentient beings. It sees existence less and less in terms of rigidity and stasis, and more and more in terms of dynamism, change and interconnectedness; in terms of an all-pervading awareness which is synonymous with love. In this way, the essential insubstantiality of the self, and of all existence, is seen as liberating rather than threatening.

The essentially insubstantial nature of the self, and of all existence, is sometimes referred to in Buddhism as *emptiness*. 'Emptiness', like 'non-self', can be a misleading term. It conjures up a sense of absence. In common parlance, we often use the word emptiness as a synonym for meaninglessness. But, emptiness, used in this Buddhist context, should convey quite the opposite of meaninglessness. It's not a nothingness, not a lack. Again, we come back to the word 'perspective'. Emptiness is a *perspective* on existence.

In the last chapter we talked about how a spacious perspective can imbue our lives with more meaning. There is something about silence, something about a vast blue sky, that seems to approximate truth. Thoreau, as we've seen, said that Walden Pond was rumoured to be bottomless because human beings need to believe in the infinite. The Buddhist perspective on life goes beyond merely bringing a sense of spaciousness into our lives. Rather, it suggests a sense of spaciousness which is unlimited and infinite, in which all 'things' rise and fall. The Buddhist perspective of emptiness offers a vision of existence which, ultimately, goes beyond all boundaries, all concepts whatsoever.

Emptiness is not some abstract theory. It doesn't present the goal of Buddhism as a chilling nothingness, nor does it imply that we should eradicate ourselves. It's a perspective which can illumine every aspect of our lives with compassion and meaning, which points to our limitless potential. Just as a sense of spaciousness may invite us to let go of our unhelpful thought patterns, a sense of emptiness invites us to live with an open palm rather than a clenched fist.

Practically speaking, this may mean any number of things. It may mean attempting to live in a more open-hearted way, challenging, for example, our belief that certain people are 'our type' and others are not. For me, one of the many advantages of being involved in the Western Buddhist Order has been the process of making friends with men and women of many nationalities, backgrounds and temperaments, some of whom I might not even have imagined getting to know when I was younger.

The perspective of emptiness invites us to be more generous, more open-handed. I vividly recall the scene at the end of a production of Molière's *The Miser* in which the miser in question, reacquainted with his hoard of money, sobs and clutches it to his chest, crooning over it as he might croon over a pet bird. The way of emptiness asks us to share our riches, let go of the clinging mentality by which we identify with our wealth - or our success, or our material possessions.

The way of emptiness invites us to become aware, too, of how we identify so tightly with our individual likes and dislikes, from the kinds of food we prefer to our sexual preferences. It also challenges us to become aware of the roles we play - whether it be doctor, patient, parent, child, victim, helper - and let go of any over-identification with that role. Such over-identification limits our potential to embrace new experience. It keeps our identity fixed.

I've always found it both challenging and refreshing when someone I know breaks out of the pigeonhole I've placed them in: the elderly lady who wrote a raunchy novel; the friend who left her miserable marriage to live with another woman; the timid schoolmate who jumped on a flight to Madrid one weekend... Such little stories present us with the truth that these selves of ours are not fixed and determined. They challenge the rigid presumption of who we think we are and who we presume we will always be. They show us that we can always embrace the new and unfamiliar.

Living with an open palm rather than a closed fist makes us aware of the extent to which we cling to particular views of ourselves. We could hold the view, for example, that we're basically useless, that there's something fundamentally wrong with us (paradoxically, such a view can give us a certain sense of security). We may have a view of ourselves as a good person or a good Buddhist. But such identification is profoundly limiting. The truth is always infinitely more complex.

In one Buddhist discourse, the *Ratnaguna-samcayagatha*, there's a memorable phrase used to describe Bodhisattvas (who could be said to be ideal Buddhists). The phrase is 'without a home they wander' and it suggests the traditional image of the wandering Buddhist monk who has literally cut all ties with home. But it has deeper implications too. The Bodhisattvas have ceased to identify not just with home and family, but with anything that normally provides security - one's body and thoughts and emotions and views. The Bodhisattvas make use of the Buddha's teaching but they do not even identify with that. They have ceased to fixate entirely, so they have no home, no resting place. They have found security in the essential emptiness and insecurity of existence.

The way of emptiness challenges us kindly and gradually to live in a more truly spontaneous way. It challenges us to loosen our tight and fearful grip on life, to let go. In letting go of the small things, we train ourselves to let go in deeper, more profound ways. At the time of death, we must let go of our grip on life itself.

There's a story by Leo Tolstoy called *The Death of Ivan Ilyich*. Ivan Ilyich is a judge, a man who has always been able to control his feelings, exert authority and judgement over others, and master events. Then he falls ill. Theoretically, he knows that he's dying but on a deeper level he's unable to accept the fact. His family and friends participate in a pretence that he's only ill, although a kindly servant, Gerasim, is able to speak the truth. With everyone but Gerasim, Ivan Ilyich assumes his habitual air of the official judge. Having lived all his life with a clenched fist rather than an open palm, he feels he cannot ask for pity and compassion - though he longs to. Seeing himself as a good man, someone who has lived so properly, someone who is 'not guilty', he cannot see why he should be punished in this way. Then one night, as he lies awake, he asks himself, 'What if I really have been wrong in the way I've lived my whole life?' He realizes he has been hiding, not just from death, but from life, that all his correctness and judgement and identification with reputation and social propriety has been a way of avoiding engaging with what is truly important in life. He realizes both that he is going to die and that his life has been a sham, and the realization appals him so utterly that he feels himself falling into a black abyss - and he screams for three entire days and nights.

Yet the terrible awareness that has dawned on him finally allows him to let go of his egotistical grip on life. In admitting that his way of living has not been right, Ivan Ilyich is finally calmed. Although his family, clustered round his bed, cannot hear him, he can ask, at least internally, for their forgiveness:

And suddenly it grew clear to him that what had been oppressing him and would not leave him was all dropping away at once from two sides, from ten sides and from all sides.

Fully and finally opening up to pain and death, he finds that they are not there any more:

He sought his accustomed fear of death and did not find it. 'Where is it? What death?'

There was no fear because there was no death.

In place of death there was light. [59]

In letting go of his habitual assumptions and rigid identity, his clinging to which manifested in a fear of death, Ivan Ilyich was finally able to find a meaning which had evaded him throughout his life.

As we begin to live more and more with an open palm rather than a clenched fist, as we progressively let go of our tendencies to fixate, cling and attach, we'll inevitably encounter a certain amount of fear. This is because we're letting go of certainty, of the known. But as we become more comfortable with that tension, the fear begins to change into something which can feel quite akin to it - excitement. We start to become curious as to what lies on the other side of our stale habits and fearful attachments. As we're about to see, when we truly let go, we let go into an intriguing mystery.

6

Meaning, Mystery, and Myth

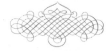

Using the figure of a raft, brothers, will I teach you the Dharma, as something to leave behind, not to take with you. [60]

IN HIS FAMOUS PARABLE OF THE RAFT, the Buddha was making the point that, just as it would be absurd for a man to cross a stretch of water by means of a raft and then load the raft on his back and carry it with him once he'd reached the further shore, so it would be ridiculous for a man to cling to the teaching of the Buddha once he'd fully realized the essence of that teaching.

The Buddha told the parable of the raft to demonstrate that his Dharma (or teaching) was a means to an end, not an end in itself. The parable addresses our literalistic tendency to become attached to teachings and models, to perceive them as the truth itself, rather than as pointers or signposts towards that truth.

In my last couple of years at school, some of my friends were gripped by a religious fever, and there was a lot of heated debate and disagreement between these friends and the heathens amongst us. Taking literally Christ's teaching that he was 'the way, the truth and the life', my friends declared that Jesus was 'THE way, THE truth and THE life', and insisted that if I didn't enter the sheepfold through his narrow gate, I would be eternally damned. To have such sweet friendships soured by religious dogmatism was a source of great frustration and disappointment to me.

So pervasive is the tendency towards dogmatism within religion that many people can be forgiven for associating such literalism with religion itself, and drawing the conclusion that meaning in life can't be found in any form of spirituality whatsoever. Yet, Buddhism has always incorporated into its teaching a critique of religion, a critique of *itself*, to ensure that Buddhist practices are always seen as means rather than as ends. All schools of Buddhism have been concerned with the practical realization of the meaning of life, as opposed to the enshrinement of a theory or dogma which expounds that meaning. Buddhism's critique of its own teachings offers a safeguard to make sure that such pragmatism remains at the forefront of teaching and practice, and that practitioners never become slaves to dogma.

That's why within Buddhism there are so many sutras and discourses, similes and metaphors aimed at rooting out literalism. This is one of the major themes of Mahayana Buddhism, for example. Such a wealth of teachings on the subject explains why Buddhism can be celebrated, to a great extent, for its lack of intolerance and dogmatism. The famous Japanese Buddhist simile of the finger pointing to the moon may stand here for all these teachings. The moon represents the truth, and the finger the teaching, and the simile demonstrates how often and how easily we mistake the finger for the moon.

The Buddha was so aware that literalism was antithetical to the realization of meaning that he declared the tendency to 'perceive rites and rituals as ends in themselves' as one of the great fetters holding us back from enlightenment. Sangharakshita equates this particular fetter with *superficiality*. It's a very appropriate word to use because the eye of literalism perceives only surfaces - and meaning doesn't reside on the surface of things. No spiritual practice will have any effect merely because it's 'spiritual'. Any spiritual practice, whether it's meditation, ritual or some altruistic activity, will be completely ineffective if we merely go through the motions. To discover meaning in life we must renounce superficiality. Meaning must be dug for.

Literalism isn't just the province of religions and the religious. It's a deep-rooted human tendency, as deep-rooted as hatred or greed. As we've seen, the Buddha taught that existence is characterized by suffering, impermanence and insubstantiality. Finding this state of affairs vastly threatening, we fixate, identify and attach to give ourselves some sense of solidity or permanence. Some of the things we attach ourselves to are our models and maps for navigating reality. The map in question may be some form of psychotherapy, a political system, a spiritual teaching... Whatever it is, we tend to identify with it to such an extent that this map for approaching reality is mistaken for reality itself. We mistake the finger for the moon.

It's as if we were to browse though a London A to Z and mistake this experience of looking at a map of London for the experience of *being* in London. It sounds absurd but it's an apt metaphor for how we fixate on the maps by which we orientate ourselves in life. Such fixation explains why, throughout the ages, men and women have been forced, often under threat of death, to assent to a particular doctrine or teaching or system of belief.

Even the best map is still a map. Sangharakshita has remarked that Buddhism is the Buddha's experience of enlightenment conceptualized and thus falsified - inevitably falsified because the Buddha's teachings are not the Buddha's actual experience of enlightenment itself. All the teachings point beyond themselves, inviting the practitioner to share the Buddha's *experience*.

It's through fear and insecurity that we hold so tightly to our models and maps. It's insecurity which compels some Christian fundamentalists to assert that the world was literally created in under a week. In asserting this, they misunderstand the value of myth and fail to see the mystery and meaning to which such a myth may be pointing.

Fear and insecurity also compel us to reach for scientific and rational models and demand that any disturbing experience be explained away by them. 'There's always a rational explanation. There's always a scientific explanation.' Such modern mantras can be very reassuring and I've used them myself - on a recent solitary retreat, for example, when I saw a strange shape beginning to manifest just below the bedroom ceiling.

But, why must our rational and scientific models explain and include all of our experience? Why must there always be a rational explanation? Perhaps, on that solitary retreat, if I'd faced up to my fear and refused to explain away the manifesting form as a combination of an optical illusion, 'Dettol' fumes and a wonky light bulb, I might have gained access to a deeper, more meaningful reality. Who knows who wanted to visit me at that time? 'There are far more things in heaven and earth, Horatio/ Than are dreamt of in your philosophy,'[61] says Hamlet to his friend, having just encountered his father's ghost. Below our mundane and rational understanding of things lies a depth of meaning which may suggest itself to us in ways which are entirely unexpected: in strange dreams perhaps, or in visions, visitations or mysterious sightings.

Unfortunately, we're so conditioned by our scientific and rational models that the very idea of ghosts, strange beasts, demons or guardian angels, may seem ridiculous. Yet, from earliest times, people have always *seen* things, whether it be ghosts, otherworldly creatures, or lights in the sky. In earlier times, such lights in the sky were perhaps called fairies. More recently, they have been apprehended as 'UFOs', reflecting our contemporary technological outlook. If we attempt to prove or refute such strange encounters scientifically, we miss the point. Even if they're not literally real, that doesn't mean they're not poetically or metaphorically real. They exist in the shadowlands, in the border areas between dreams and waking life, between conscious and unconscious experience. They appear in the twilight, in the fading light between day and night, where boundaries are blurred. They are there in the corners of our minds where our usual models and explanations don't quite reach. They're the strange weeds that creep through the cracks in our certainties, manifestations of the truth that no model can fully explain reality. Fairies, ghosts, UFOs, the grumpy little troll who lived near the retreat centre in Wales, and who was seen by many retreatants - such things never quite disappear from human life. They defeat our attempts to control reality.

Because we do want to control reality. We long for certainties. Unfortunately, if we're truly searching for meaning in life, we need to give up on certainties (other than death and taxes). The grumpy little troll who lived near the retreat centre in Wales insists that life is very, very mysterious indeed. If we just contemplate our own hand for a while, in the way we might have done as tiny children, we realize that nothing can explain the baffling mystery of our embodiment and our human consciousness. As we saw in the last chapter, if we contemplate any *thing* seriously for any length of time, we realize that it is in reality an infinitely complex amalgamation of parts and conditions. It's essentially mysterious. Yet, unhappy with such a mystery, we once again literalize our experience by becoming attached to our labels for things.

I remember walking down the road in Glasgow and watching a beautiful collie dog rush towards a mother and her little boy. The boy was utterly captivated by this golden vision bounding towards him and excitedly cried to his mother, 'Mammy, what's that?' His mother gave the dog a cursory and unimpressed glance. 'It's a *dug*,' she said. Mystery explained.

Dug. Cat. Man. Woman. Vase. Glass. Our labels for things, necessary though they may be, belie the mystery in front of us. If we want to bring more meaning into our lives, we must go beneath the convenient label which is all surface, and only serves provisionally to categorize what's there. Any good painter or artist attempts to ignore the label, to go below the surface of things, to do something more than merely reproduce a photographic likeness of a person or object or landscape. When we admire a bowl of fruit by Cézanne, or a vase of flowers by Van Gogh, we're taken below our mundane way of perceiving things into a deeper, more meaningful reality. The painter Kandinsky said that Cézanne, in his paintings, managed to make a living thing out of a teacup, breathed animation and a mysterious life into objects, was 'endowed with the gift of divining the inner life in everything'.[62] The literal mind, however, is happy with the label.

The enlightened mind has been likened to a mirror to which nothing sticks. By contrast, there's something very sticky about the literal mind. Thoughts and concepts and images rise and fall in our awareness. If that awareness can be likened to the sky, and the thoughts and concepts going through our mind to the clouds, then we identify closely with the clouds. We create stories around them and take those stories literally. We *stick* to them. When a dark cloud wanders through our mind, we give a name to it and, in naming it, believe that it represents a fixed and permanent truth. We literalize it, identify with it, say that 'we are depressed'.

Behind all our thoughts and concepts, like a radiantly beautiful sky, lies the vast mystery of human awareness, the miracle of aliveness. If we could only embrace this mystery, identify (if we are to identify with anything) with the awareness itself rather than with the objects constantly rising and falling within that awareness, life could seem so much more meaningful - and mysterious. But, it's a mystery that seems difficult to perceive. It seems that normally we can't or won't see it. We can't see the wood for the trees. We can't see the sky for the clouds. We stick to drifting thoughts and concepts and make realities of them. We take them literally. Life can easily appear meaningless because we're looking for meaning in the wrong place - on the surface of things.

One way in which we can bring more meaning into our lives is by a more creative use of thoughts and concepts. As we've seen, we can counteract our tendency to identify with thoughts and allow them to proliferate, by bringing more pauses and empty spaces into our lives. Through meditation, we can let go of attachment to passing thoughts and bring more awareness to bear on our experience. Thinking is sometimes used in meditation, to reflect on the nature of

Reality for example, but such thought is used consciously and with the aim of accessing deeper levels of meaning. Through meditation, we begin to see the ephemeral nature of our thinking, to see that thoughts and concepts are not fixed realities. In other words, meditation enables us to take our passing thoughts less literally, less *seriously*.

We can also be more creative in our use of concepts in discussion or communication, perhaps using them more playfully, as Sangharakshita suggests:

Concepts had therefore better be treated as symbols, the value of which lies not in their literal meaning so much as their suggestiveness. They should be handled in the spirit not of logic but of poetry; not pushed hither and thither with grim calculation like pieces on a chessboard, but tossed lightly, playfully in the air like a juggler's multicoloured balls. [63]

Sangharakshita makes the same point when he tells us that the term 'play words', meaning concepts, occurs again and again in Milarepa's songs (Milarepa was a famous Tibetan yogi whose teachings were spontaneously and joyfully expressed in song):

By calling concepts 'play words' he [Milarepa] means he no longer takes them as referring to fixed or absolute realities. [64]

We need concepts to get through the day, to communicate with one another, to differentiate a cat from a piece of cake, but the problem is that, unlike Milarepa, we tend to see concepts as fixed or absolute realities. But Reality can never be absolutely explained in concepts. That's why, far from there always being a rational explanation for everything, there is ultimately never a rational explanation for *anything*. The rational explanation is not the reality itself. It can only point the way.

This isn't to deny the importance of clear thinking. As we've seen in a previous chapter, conceptual tools are of vital importance for our spiritual journey. It's our literalistic approach to them that's the problem. Our inability to see concepts as play words gets in the way of so much meaningful discussion or debate. When a discussion founders or descends into bad-tempered argument, it's very often because of literalism.

Let's take a hypothetical example. White and Black are both Buddhist practitioners. Black is in the habit of taking some brandy every night before bed. White tells Black that their teacher once said that the consumption of alcohol and a spiritual life are incompatible. Black says that the brandy is authentically medicinal. White says that brandy is alcohol and their teacher said it was incompatible with a spiritual life. Black says that their teacher also said that one should pay more heed to the spirit of the teaching than the letter. White asks if that means the letter is not important. Black says that the spirit is *more* important and she is *not* going to stop having her nightly brandy. White asks if this also means that Black is going to renounce the spiritual life. Black says that White is being literal-minded and self-righteous. And so it goes on...

White is probably not taking into consideration the fact that the teacher said what he said at a particular time, in a particular context to a particular set of people. Too often we latch on to a concept, idea or teaching and believe it to be literally true for all people, at all times and in all places. We take things out of context and miss the subtlety of what's being said. But perhaps Black is being literal-minded when she cites her teacher's exhortation to heed the spirit of the teaching over the letter. We are all masterful at taking any idea, any teaching, and using a literal understanding of it to support our ego and desires. Perhaps Black wants to justify an accelerating brandy habit. Whatever the truth of the matter, Black and

White are using the teachings as fixed, literal realities to beat each other into submission. Complexity and subtlety will never get a look in.

Literalism is particularly prevalent in ethical debate because ethical rules are so often cited as absolutes. Yet in Buddhism, ethical precepts are guidelines, not commandments. This doesn't mean that these guidelines are merely optional or that they shouldn't be taken very seriously. But in Buddhism, more ethically appropriate actions are termed 'skilful', and more inappropriate ones 'unskilful'. Thus, ethics is a craft to be learned rather than a set of rules (inscribed on stone tablets and handed down by a fearsome authority) to be followed. The latter divides the mind into good and evil, black and white, and can, thus, more easily foster a dangerous literalism.

All of this doesn't mean that we shouldn't defend, vigorously, what we perceive to be true or ethical. But, if we can relax our fierce grip on our views, if we can use concepts, thoughts and ideas to play together and get at the truth, rather than using them to defeat the enemy in some grim chess match, our communication will become both more enjoyable and more meaningful. Meaning in life can't be cultivated without a sense of humour, and having a sense of humour is a way of finding a less literalistic and more realistic perspective on existence. I'm not advocating being frivolous, cynical or diffident about life, but letting go of the pride which comes with attaching ourselves so firmly to our roles and preferences, our arguments, views and concepts.

In his film *The Great Dictator*, Charlie Chaplin parodied Adolf Hitler, a man who perhaps exemplified more than any other the danger of becoming attached to concepts. Chaplin's 'Adenoid Hynkel' addresses a Fascist rally with mechanical, robotic movements, and a series of absurd, strangulated sounds and guttural shouts, which expose the meaninglessness of Hitler's oratory and the hateful, literalistic perspective which lay behind it. In a later scene, Hynkel, alone in his study, removes a huge globe from its stand and begins to play with it. The globe becomes a balloon, the Fascist dictator flirtatiously waltzing with it, moving with a dainty and balletic grace which is the comic antithesis of the frozen, rigid mindset which has led him to seek world domination. With his uniquely comic perspective, Chaplin reveals Hitler's horrifying megalomania and transforms it into a delightfully playful dance.

It's significant that the spiritual life of the Bodhisattva, the ideal Buddhist, is said to be a playful life. This doesn't detract from the seriousness of their task. Quite the contrary. Bodhisattvas have a why to live for and pursue their vocation with seriousness and determination - but also with a spontaneous joy. They don't adopt the grim-lipped expression of the martyr when helping others. In them, having ceased to identify with concepts and ego, having learned to live with an open palm rather than a clenched fist, meaning and joy are combined.

Throughout this book, we've seen how perspective and meaning are interlinked. Literalism leads one to a narrow and superficial perspective on life which is the enemy of meaning. The poet William Blake equated literalism with what he called 'single vision', by which he meant a blinkered perspective on life which sees only surfaces. But, Blake saw the world with 'double vision', that is, he perceived the surface, mundane reality of life but was also able to see through it to a deeper, more meaningful reality. (Indeed, his conception of how to perceive the world aright went on to include 'threefold' and 'fourfold' vision.) Here is his response to a question he imagines being asked:

'When the sun rises, do you not see a round disk of fire some-what like a Guinea?' 'O no, no, I see an Innumerable company of the Heavenly host crying "Holy, Holy, Holy is the Lord God almighty".[65]

Blake could see the sun perfectly well in its factual day-to-day aspect as a round disk, but he was also able to see it more poetically, more *meaningfully*. He didn't just see the coin. He wasn't fooled by appearances. Neither did he just see the choir of angels (which would be a form of madness). He had the double vision which could perceive both the literal reality and its deeper, more mysterious significance. The job of the poet, the artist and the spiritual practitioner, in fact the job of *anyone* who is intent on bringing meaning into their life, is to cultivate this double vision.

One way we can do this is by becoming involved in a creative pursuit which takes us below the surface, beneath the labels and the conceptual models - reading or writing poetry or fiction, playing or listening to music, painting or looking at pictures. The sun could be described as a body of gaseous matter consisting of hydrogen, helium and other elements, with a surface temperature of 5,500 degrees Celsius, 92,960,000 miles distant from the Earth. Philip Larkin wrote a poem called *Solar* which I think describes it more accurately. The poem begins:

Suspended lion face
Spilling at the centre
Of an unfurnished sky
How still you stand,
And how unaided
Single stalkless flower
You pour unrecompensed.[66]

Larkin breathes animation into dead matter. Like Cézanne, he seems to divine an inner life in the object of his perception. Through his eyes we see the sun in a more mysterious and meaningful way, through a series of images which suggest the heavenly body's inexhaustible generosity. When I read the poem I'm reminded of an infinitely compassionate golden Buddha responding to human need with an eternally open palm.

When we speak of trying to find the meaning of life, the implication can be that there's some literal answer out there to be discovered. In the first of the series of Douglas Adams's comic radio shows and novels, *The Hitchhiker's Guide to the Galaxy*, a group of hyper-intelligent beings demand to learn the Answer to the Ultimate Question of Life, the Universe and Everything, and they build a computer, Deep Thought, for the purpose. It takes Deep Thought seven and a half million years to come up with the answer, which turns out to be 42. (Unfortunately, the Ultimate Question remains unknown.) A great poem or painting offers no such certainties, no literal answers. It takes us deeper and deeper into the mystery, into the very heart of the sun.

But we human beings aren't at ease with mystery. The literalistic mind demands definite answers, insists that the mystery be solved. (The answer is 42. It's a *dug*.) We resist fluidity, dynamism and impermanence, and seek to substantiate, explain and control. It's very hard for us to understand literalism or catch the literal mind at work because our world and our mind are so conditioned by it. Things and thoughts and people seem so substantial, so concrete. Words such as 'real' and 'true' invariably mean literally real, literally true - not poetically true.

Buddhist teachings, though they may be couched in precise conceptual terms (although others are more mythic

or poetic), are attempting to do what an effective poem
or painting is attempting to do. They are pointing beyond
literalism, beyond superficiality and certainties, to a deeper
sense of meaning, a great mystery. The Buddhist, like the poet,
is trying not to solve this mystery but to embrace it. He or
she is attempting to see through mundane reality to a reality
which is more beautiful, more meaningful - and yet more
ephemeral and transient. In the famous Buddhist text called
the *Diamond Sutra*§*, the Buddha reminds us how we should
perceive this fleeting life:

As stars, a fault of vision, as a lamp,
A mock show, dew drops, or a bubble,
A dream, a lightning flash, or cloud,
So should one view what is conditioned.[67]

Truly, our lives are as insubstantial as dreams, and one
way we can bring more meaning into our lives is to pay
more attention to our dreams. Our dream experience tends
to be far less literal and far more fluid than our waking life.
We shape-shift between roles and characters, for example.
Objects often have a symbolic or metaphorical quality.
Our dream experience is less literally true than our waking
experience, but sometimes it may be more poetically true. I
had a dream recently in which I was at a Buddhist gathering,
standing by a river in a vaguely mythical landscape, deeply
content. I became aware that I was dreaming, and I also
became aware that this dream, and the state of mind I was
inhabiting in this dream state, was more true, more meaningful, than my waking life. I also realized that, in a few
minutes, I'd have to wake up, and at this last thought I felt
extremely distraught.

---

§* The theme of the *Diamond Sutra* is the profound implications of emptiness and insubstantiality. The
Chinese *Diamond Sutra* is, in the words of the British Library, 'the earliest complete survival of a dated,
printed book'. It was printed in 868CE.

Another way we can get beneath the superficial, literal aspect of existence is to cultivate the mythical. Myths are narrative patterns which give meaning and purpose to our lives. They take the most significant aspects of human experience, such as birth, death, initiation, our relationship to the divine, leaving home, falling in love, and so on, and weave them into a story which is applicable to all peoples at all times. Myths are not literal truths but eternal truths which transcend time. They provide the invisible framework to our lives, and without a significant myth to live by, our lives will feel meaningless. We will have no way of fitting the chaos of our experience into a meaningful, narrative context.

About twenty-five years ago I was living in a cottage in the Highlands, snow-bound and in a state of painful confusion. My life felt meaningless. I'd been living in a Christian community and had made many good friends, but I'd realized that I didn't believe in God and that Christianity wasn't for me, so I had left the community abruptly, letting many people down in the process. I'd been investigating Buddhism but I didn't quite believe that I could adopt, wholesale, what seemed to me at that time to be an alien way of life. In that painful state, I found myself constantly referring to a particular novel (which was also made into a movie): *One Flew Over the Cuckoo's Nest*.

The story tells of Randle McMurphy, an anarchic criminal who is confined in a mental institution. McMurphy challenges the authorities and, with a combined sense of mischief and genuine concern, also challenges the passivity and despair of the other inmates. He befriends a native American, 'Chief' Bromden, whom he originally believed to be deaf and dumb, but who has merely been biding his time until the day he can find the courage to break out. Together they plan to escape. But eventually McMurphy's rebellion is crushed and he is lobotomized. It's this tragedy which finally impels the Chief to break out of the institution.

Looking back on it now, I think that what the book did was to help me bridge the gap between two narratives, one in which I could no longer believe, and another to which I hadn't quite committed myself. *One Flew Over the Cuckoo's Nest* was not, strictly speaking, a myth but, like the very best novels, Ken Kesey's story had mythical qualities which brought some much needed order and understanding to my life. To over-simplify, although I wasn't conscious of this at the time, to me McMurphy represented Christianity and the Chief represented Buddhism. McMurphy was destroyed, but his martyrdom impelled the Chief to act and gain his freedom. In identifying with the characters, in turning the story over and over in my mind and reliving it, I felt able to summon up the courage to leap over what seemed like a dangerous chasm.

Many of us have grown up comparatively bereft of a mythical perspective on our lives. One of the reasons for this is the contemporary distrust of the mythical. It shows how bound we are by the literal and the rational that we can talk in terms of '*just* a myth' or, 'only a myth'. Even those who subscribe to particular myths (e.g. the Resurrection of Christ or the Old Testament Creation myth) often feel the need to take those myths literally, unaware that myth operates on a different level from the literal. In bringing the mythical into our lives we are, again, attempting to perceive reality with double vision in Blake's sense. We are perfectly aware of mundane, day-to-day reality but we're also attempting to contextualize that reality within a more meaningful narrative. Because, ultimately, the mythical, far from being 'just the mythical', is more truly meaningful than the mundane.

This distrust and devaluing of myth coincides with the collapse of any shared myth. For centuries, Christianity provided, for entire populations, a shared public myth, a narrative to which everybody subscribed, with images, rituals and feast days which were, until the Reformation at least, collectively recognized. In many countries this is no longer the case, and many people now have to search desperately amongst the fragments of myth and legend for stories that suit their purposes. There is one thing for certain: we must have some kind of mythic context in our lives to bring some order to the chaos of sensations and images and ideas in our minds. For, although we are rational creatures who tend to literalize our experience, we're also mythical beings who are hungry for a prevailing story, who long for a more meaningful reality. So, we pick and choose amongst the minutiae of our culture, amongst the novels, movies, music and TV programmes, looking for traces of the lost mythical realm for which we yearn. In this way we cobble together some story to live by, some personal myth.

These private narratives, however meaningful, will always be limited. Even the best of our 'personal myths' need to be subsumed into something greater. *One Flew Over the Cuckoo's Nest* was not a profound enough narrative for me to be able to order my life around it. (I doubt if it would have been able to sustain me on my death bed, for example.) As we've seen in an earlier chapter, the private and personal myth is a contradiction in terms. If discovering meaning in life is, as I've argued, synonymous with going beyond self-concern, the myth to which we subscribe must be a public myth, a shared myth. A myth can't exist just for our own benefit, can't just refer to ourselves. Perhaps a particular myth can no longer encompass the values of a whole society, but our personal stories can be incorporated into a myth which resonates with a significant number of people who share our ideals.

'And here stands man', said the philosopher Friedrich Nietzsche, 'stripped of myth, eternally starving, in the midst of all the past ages, digging and scrabbling for roots, even if he must dig for them in the most remote antiquities.'[68] Nietzsche misunderstood Buddhism, seeing it merely as a kind of courageous Stoicism. Perhaps if he'd had access to more Buddhist texts, and better translations, he might have conceded that the legend of the Buddha might have supplied the profound narrative which he felt mankind was crying out for.

Buddhism, of course, is much more than the legend of the Buddha. What we call Buddhism incorporates a vast variety of practices, an ethical framework, the experience of spiritual community, and so on... But underpinning all of this is the life and experience of Siddhartha, who became the Awakened One, the Buddha; who, according to legend, after witnessing the four great sights, renounced the life of a great warrior to become a conqueror of the self. A Buddhist, in attempting to discover meaning in life, re-enacts this story. This is not a literal re-enactment, although some aspects of the Buddha's story may coincide with our own experience, but a re-enactment based on our commitment to the Buddhist path. In committing ourselves thus, we perceive all of our life experience within the context of the myth of the Buddha's life.

With its themes of the confrontation of suffering, the renunciation of violence, the rejection of both hedonism and self-mortification, and the arising of supreme altruism and love, it's a myth that seems appropriate for our age, particularly immersed, as we are, in financial insecurity and a terrible environmental crisis. The Buddha's life gives us a narrative of personal responsibility. There is no God to defer to, cry out for, or blame. The myth of the Buddha challenges us to re-enact Siddhartha's experience under the tree of enlightenment. We are capable of discovering the meaning he discovered. We can overcome what he overcame. We too can become Buddhas.

This sublime state can only be brought into being by the choices we make and the actions we perform in our daily lives. The great peak of enlightenment must be approached by way of the next small step, by way of the little details, and in concluding our search for meaning in life, it's to such details that we now turn our attention.

Conclusion: Everything that Lives is Holy[69]

AT THE BEGINNING OF THIS BOOK I quoted Leo Tolstoy, who, in the midst of a mid-life crisis, asked himself some very basic questions: Why should we live? Why should we do anything? Is there any meaning in life which death doesn't undo? In the subsequent chapters we have looked at different ways in which we might bring meaning into our lives, different ways in which Tolstoy's questions might be answered. An awareness of suffering as a universal phenomenon; a *why* to live for and a commitment to a concrete task beyond mere self-concern; loving-kindness; a sense of spaciousness; relaxing our hold on habit, attachment and fixation; cultivating both 'double vision' and a sense of the mythical: these are the themes through which we have explored the question of meaning.

We have also seen that our sense of meaning *in* life and our perspective on life are inextricably connected. A Buddhist's perspective on existence, which we may call 'right view', is a reflection, however faint, of the Perfect Vision which the Buddha experienced after his enlightenment, a vision of complete egolessness. Meaning in life, for a Buddhist, is found by moving towards egolessness, and it's with this underlying perspective, this right view, that we attempt to transform every aspect of our lives. Ideally, it's with right view that we approach the big questions in life, and also life's small, daily tasks.

Without the vision to see beyond self-centredness, those daily tasks will seem meaningless. Without tasks to ground ourselves, our vision will remain abstract and unmanageable. Without such tasks, too, we may find ourselves swamped by life's big questions - or even use them as a distraction. Cue the poet Roger McGough:

Survivor

Everyday
I think about dying.
About disease, starvation,
violence, terrorism, war,
the end of the world.

It helps
keep my mind off things. [70]

We may reflect upon and ponder the meaning of life. We may have visionary experiences in meditation. We may genuinely feel that we want to alleviate the suffering of all sentient beings. But ultimately, as we've seen, it's only through the next small task, the next kindly act, that we can actualize our vision and access true meaning. And these small tasks themselves can be broken down into small details. Meaning in life consists in the details, as well as in the vision.

So, altruism is rooted in the particular reports we have to fill in for work, work which earns the cash to feed the kids. Love manifests itself when we're moved by the unique way a friend or child or partner bends over a book. We experience a delightful sense of spaciousness when an individual place calls to us on an individual day, and we find ourselves on a particular beach at dusk, staring at a grey sea and a darkening sky. It is never Art in the abstract that moves us, but always a particular painting or poem that takes us below the surface of things to a deeper sense of meaning. An awareness of suffering comes down to this particular person with this particular illness living in this particular home, sitting in this particular armchair and giving us this particular opportunity to practise patience. A step on the journey towards egolessness is made through lifting *this* spoon to *this* person's mouth.

Our sense of purpose and vision gives meaning to the concrete tasks to which we've committed ourselves, and those tasks in turn give meaning to the particular details they involve. But it works the other way too. Paying attention to the little details gives meaning to the tasks, and that strengthens our sense of purpose and vision.

As we saw in chapter 4, a sense of meaning in life can also come from paying attention to the things we do *in between* the seemingly more important things in life: the mundane actions of folding our clothes, waiting for the bus, chopping the vegetables, washing the dishes, sewing on a button... Much of our lives is occupied with such details, and if we gloss over them in order to get on with things that seem more important, opportunities for appreciation, enjoyment and even illumination are missed.

The Buddhist practice of mindfulness consists of developing an awareness of both vision and detail. The Buddha saw this practice as so important that he referred to it in his very last words: 'with mindfulness, strive on'. Mindfulness involves being aware of our purpose in life, of our why to live for. It also involves trying to bring as much awareness as we can to the day-to-day, and the minute-to-minute, tasks of our lives. Very often, these details are lost or obscured because we're elsewhere. We can eat a whole meal, for example, and realize afterwards that we haven't tasted a thing. We just haven't been paying attention to what we've been doing. We've been regretting the past or considering the future. Very rarely are we fully present to what's in front of us at any given moment.

The practice of mindfulness counteracts this deep-rooted tendency to distraction. Consciously and deliberately, we attempt to bring awareness to all aspects of our lives. We try to become more aware of our bodies, for example, through yoga, massage, Alexander technique, some form of regular exercise, or just by the increasing power of mindfulness as a positive habit. Similarly, we try to become more aware of our thoughts and emotions, not as a solipsistic exercise, but as a way of bringing more choice into our lives. ('Do I want to follow this thought?' 'Have I noticed how I always react with this emotion?') We also try to become more mindful of other people. This may involve, for example, really listening. I had one friend who was particularly good at this. It was a very attractive characteristic. I always had a sense that when I was talking, he really listened to me, really gave me his full attention, and I came to love that little furrow on his brow as he considered what I was saying.

One of the great qualities of the Buddha was his mindfulness of others. It's said that when the Buddha gave someone his attention, it was with an 'elephant look'. That is, like an elephant, he never just turned his head towards somebody, but his entire body. His whole *being* exerted an undivided, concentrated attention. He was overwhelmingly present to whoever was with him. He also seemed to know how to talk to a huge variety of people, from kings and queens to craftsmen and servants. Furthermore, he seemed to know exactly what any individual might need at any given time, in order to take the next step on the spiritual path.

In practising mindfulness we're also trying to become more alive to our sensual experience. We're trying to become more aware of sights and sounds and smells, of what we touch, what we taste and what our mind perceives. The more mindful we are, the more beauty and simple enjoyment we bring into our lives. When we're unmindful, we're living less fully, less beautifully. We're less alive and less awake. Mindfulness also gives us far more choice, more freedom to decide which sensual experience to dwell upon, which to relinquish.

The practice of mindfulness also deepens our awareness and appreciation of objects, our environment and the world around us. This is useful on a very practical level. We're less likely to trip over the furniture, for example. We can navigate a busy street more safely. The road to enlightenment, after all, must begin with the ability to recall where we put our walking boots. But the more effectively we practise mindfulness, and the more aware we become of the objective world, the more we're able to access the meaning and the mystery that resides in the objects of our perception.

Such an awareness can be particularly enhanced by the regular practice of the mindfulness of breathing meditation. In this practice, we attempt to become absorbed in the breath. We try gently to let go of mental distraction and come back, again and again, to the physical sensations of the breathing. The meditation practice is a training in mindfulness, and those new to the practice often notice that after the meditation, colours often seem that little bit sharper, objects that little bit more defined. As the enveloping filter of ego becomes a little thinner, we're able to see more clearly what's in front of us. A Buddhist is like the poet or the artist in this respect. As we saw in the last chapter, we're attempting to go beyond the superficial labels, attempting to see into the heart of things.

Imagine being so present to the world around you that absolutely everything is imbued with the radiant power of mindfulness. This must have been the experience of the Buddha. Residing in a permanent state of egolessness, he must have perceived everything as filled with a meaningful and mysterious presence. We may even have had a reflection of such an experience ourselves, albeit a very faint one...

Perhaps you're in a favourite landscape and your mind is calm and collected. You feel relaxed and content, your usual jumble of thoughts not jostling for attention. Your mind feels spacious, occupied only by your environment and the sky above you. As you stand there, your life, at that moment, seems particularly meaningful, particularly directed. And then, perhaps, you regard some object with your full and undivided awareness - a gull, a cloud, a rock... And, just for a moment, you are thrilled to your core by the strange miracle of it.

Perhaps this is what William Blake meant when he said that 'everything that lives is holy'. Not just everything that lives, but everything that exists. Even the litter on the ground can seem beautiful, meaningful or mysterious when illuminated by the power of real awareness, real mindfulness. Even a fragment of litter can reassure us that there's meaning in life.

Buddhism can provide us with a perspective on existence which imbues our lives with meaning. It can provide answers to the questions that so tormented Leo Tolstoy and the

Buddha, and torment any human being who has contemplated the true significance of life. But, the answers that Buddhism provides are not literal ones. Sometimes they may not even seem particularly comforting. Buddhism does not explain a mystery but helps us to embrace that mystery. It helps us to live without certainties whilst challenging us to be confident that the more we move beyond self-concern, the more meaningful and beautiful our lives will become. In this respect, even the seeming senselessness of so much suffering, although demanding ever deeper levels of compassion, may begin to assume a mysterious, if inexplicable, significance.

Many years ago I had one of the strongest dreams of my life. I dreamt about a piece of litter lying in the street - the corner of a gold Benson and Hedges fag packet. In the dream, the gold fragment began to glow. As I looked at it, it was as if the whole of the universe was contained in this fragment. It was shining with meaning, illumined with a kind of laughing wisdom. The piece of litter seemed to contain the universe.

A couple of years after I'd had that dream, I'd just said my farewells to a friend who was dying. He was someone with a great and partly unrealized potential, a kind and intensely playful character who had inspired me hugely - and he was going to die young. His death seemed pointless, even tragic. On the way out of his gate I noticed a fragment of litter by the gatepost - the corner of a gold Benson and Hedges fag packet, winking at me mischievously in the sun.

Bibliography

These are the texts and films I have particularly drawn upon in the writing of this book:

- Sir Edwin Arnold, *The Light of Asia*, Windhorse Publications, Birmingham, 1999.
- Victor Frankel, *Man's Search for Meaning*, Rider, London, 2004.
- Patrick Harpur, *Daimonic Reality*, Penguin Arkana, 1995. Unfortunately this extremely intelligent book about "other worldly encounters" and literalism is out of print (ISBN: 0-670-85569-3). Harpur's ideas particularly influenced chapter 7 of this book.
- Ken Kesey, *One Flew Over the Cuckoo's Nest*, Picador, London, 1973.
- Rollo May, *The Cry for Myth*, W.W. Norton & Company, NY, 1991.
- Adam Philips and Barbara Taylor, *On Kindness*, Hamish Hamilton, London, 2008.
- J.D. Salinger, *The Catcher in the Rye*, Penguin, London, 1958.
- Sangharakshita, *The Three Jewels*, Windhorse Publications, Birmingham, 1977.
- Sangharakshita, *The Buddha's Noble Eightfold Path*, Windhorse Publications, Birmingham, 2007.
- Sangharakshita, *Wisdom Beyond Words*, Windhorse Publications, Birmingham, 1993.
- Sangharakshita, *Crossing the Stream*, Windhorse Publications, Birmingham, 1987. Unfortunately this book is out of print (ISBN: 0-904766-78-0) but a pdf version is available at www.sangharakshita.org.
- Subhuti, *The Mythic Context* (a series of three transcribed lectures), Padmaloka Books, Norwich, 2001.
- Leo Tolstoy, *The Death of Ivan Ilyich*, translated by Anthony Briggs, Penguin, London, 2006.

- *One Flew Over the Cuckoo's Nest* directed by Milos Forman, 1975.
- *Ikiru* directed by Akira Kurosawa, 1952.

Notes and References

1. Woody Allen, 'My Speech to the Graduates' in *Complete Prose*, Picador, London, 1992, p.361.
2. James Thomson, *The City of Dreadful Night*, Canongate Books, Edinburgh, 1993, p.56
3. William Wordsworth, *The Prelude*, Oxford University Press, Oxford, 1970.
4. Ibid.
5. William Shakespeare, *Macbeth*, Act V Sc. 5, Routledge, London, 1988, p.154.
6. Thomas Hobbes, *Leviathan*, Penguin English Library, London, 1981.
7. Leo Tolstoy, *A Confession*, trans. Aylmer Maude, Oxford University Press, Oxford, 1971, p.24.
8. Alexander Solzhenitsyn, *Harvard Commencement Address*, 1978.
9. Alexander Solzhenitsyn, *Warning to the West*, Farrar, Straus and Giroux, New York 1976.
10. Julian of Norwich. *Revelations of Divine Love*, Penguin, London, 1966, p.68.
11. Sir Edwin Arnold, *The Light of Asia*, Windhorse Publications, Birmingham, 1999, p.31 (ISBN: I 899579 19 2).
12. Ibid, p.33.
13. Ibid, p.33.
14. Ibid, p.67.
15. Ibid.
16. T.S. Eliot, 'The Four Quartets' in *Collected Poems*, Faber & Faber, London, 1975, p.201.
17. Rollo May, *The Cry for Myth*, W.W. Norton & Company, New York, 1991, p.114.
18. Charles Dickens quoted by John Forster in *The Life of Charles Dickens*. Book 8, Section 2, Everyman, London, 1923.
19. William Nicholson, *Shadowlands,* 1985.
20. J.D. Salinger, *The Catcher in the Rye*, Penguin, London, 1958, p.160.
21. Ibid, p.200.
22. Ibid, p.219.
23. Ibid, p.109.

24. Spinoza, 'Ethics', quoted by Victor E. Frankel in, *Man's Search for Meaning*, Rider, London, 2004, p.82.

25. Victor E. Frankl, *Man's Search for Meaning*, Rider, London, 2004, p.117.

26. Ibid, p.75.

27. Ibid, p.115.

28. Kurosawa in conversation with the actor, Takashi Shimura quoted in the notes to the BFI edition of the DVD, *Ikiru*, directed by Akira Kurosawa, 1952.

29. *Ikiru*, directed by Akira Kurosawa, 1952.

30. Ibid.

31. Tolstoy, op. cit., p.42.

32. Allen Ginsberg, *Howl*, City Lights Books, San Francisco, 1985, p.9.

33. Nagabodhi quoted in, *Dhardo Rimpoche: A Celebration*, ed. Sara Hagel, Windhorse Publications, Birmingham, 2000, p.11.

34. Vijayamala quoted in *Dhardo Rimpoche: A Celebration*, ibid, p.20.

35. Dhardo Rimpoche quoted in, Suvajra, *The Wheel and the Diamond*, Windhorse Publications, Birmingham, 1991, p.128. (ISBN: 0-904766-48-9)

36. Germaine Greer, 'Obsession' in, *The Female Eunuch*, Paladin, London, 1971, p.169.

37. Richard Dawkins, *The Selfish Gene*, Oxford University Press, Oxford, 1989, p.3.

38. Adam Philips and Barbara Taylor, *On Kindness,* Hamish Hamilton, London, 2008.

39. A.N. Wilson, *God's Funeral*, Abacus, London, 2003.

40. Sangharakshita, *Who is the Buddha?*, Windhorse Publications, Birmingham, 1994, p.72.

41. Edmund White, *My Lives*, Bloomsbury, London, 2005.

42. W.S. Gilbert quoted in, Peter McWilliams, *Love 101*, Prelude Press, Los Angeles, 1997, p.92.

43. Santideva, *The Bodhicaryavatara*, trans. Kate Crosby and Andrew Skilton, verses 17 and 18, Windhorse Publications, Birmingham, 2002, p.28.

44. Sangharakshita, *Crossing the Stream*, Windhorse Publications, Birmingham, 1997, p.95.

45. *Dhammapada*, trans. Sangharakshita, Windhorse Publications, Birmingham, 2001, p.72.

46. Ryokan, *One Robe, One Bowl*, trans. John Stevens, Weatherhill, New

Notes and References

York and Tokyo, 1986, p.43.

47. William Shakespeare, 'Hamlet', Act IV Scene 4 in, *Complete Works*, Clarendon Press, Oxford, 1998, p.689.

48. Ibid, Act III Scene 1, p.670.

49. 'The Uraga Sutta of the Sutta Nipata', Verse 8 quoted in, Bhikkhu Nanananda, *Concept and Reality*, Buddhist Publication Society, Sri Lanka, 1986, p.29.

50. From a Dhamma talk by Ajahn Sumedho of Amaravati Monastery, *Noticing Space*, printed in a pamphlet for free distribution by Ms. Sila Amonvatana, p.1.

51. Socrates, quoted in Plato, *Apology*, ed. James J. Helm, Bolchazy-Carducci Publishers, USA, 1999.

52. Henry David Thoreau, *Waldon: Or, Life in the Woods*, Shambhala, Boston, 2004.

53. Ibid.

54. George Mackay Brown, 'The Poet' in, *The Collected Poems of George Mackay Brown*, John Murray, London, 2005, p.45.

55. Sangharakshita, *A Guide to the Buddhist Path*, Windhorse Publications, Birmingham, 1990, p.35.

56. Arnold, op. cit., p.129.

57. Sangharakshita, *Crossing the Stream*, op. cit., p.198.

58. Sangharakshita, *Wisdom Beyond Words*, Windhorse Publications, Birmingham, 1993, p.129.

59. Leo Tolstoy, 'The Death of Ivan Illyich', trans. Louise and Aylmer Maude, in *Ivan Illyich and Hadji Murad*, Oxford University Press, 1935, p.73.

60. Pali Canon, Majjhima Nikaya 22, Alagaddupama Sutta.

61. Shakespeare, *Hamlet*, op. cit., Act I Scene 5, p.662.

62. Wassily Kandinsky, *Concerning the Spiritual in Art*, Dover, New York, 1977.

63. Sangharakshita, *The Three Jewels*, Windhorse Publications, Birmingham, 1977, p.54.

64. Sangharakshita, *The Yogi's Joy*, Windhorse Publications, Birmingham 2006, p.74.

65. William Blake, *Complete Writings*, Oxford University Press, Oxford, 1992, p.617.

66. Philip Larkin, 'Solar' in, *Collected Poems*, Faber & Faber, London, p.159.

67. 'The Diamond Sutra', quoted in Sangharakshita, *Wisdom Beyond Words*, op. cit., p.61.

68. Friederich Nietzsche, *The Birth of Tragedy from the Spirit of Music*, Penguin, London, 1993, p.110.

69. William Blake, 'Visions of the Daughters of Albion' in, *Complete Writings*, op. cit., p.195.

70. Roger McGough, 'Survivor' in, *Collected Poems*, Penguin, London, 2004, p.355.

All effort has been made to procure permission to quote or use the following:

Page 103: Poem by Philip Larkin, 'Solar' in, *Collected Poems*, Faber & Faber, London, p. 159.

Page 112: Poem by Roger McGough, 'Survivor' in, *Collected Poems*, Penguin, London, 2004, p. 355.

About Windhorse Publications

Windhorse Publications is a Buddhist publishing house, staffed by practising Buddhists. We place great emphasis on producing books of high quality, accessible and relevant to those interested in Buddhism at whatever level. Drawing on the whole range of the Buddhist tradition, our books include translations of traditional texts, commentaries, books that make links with Western culture and ways of life, biographies of Buddhists, and works on meditation.

As a charitable institution we welcome donations to help us continue our work. We also welcome manuscripts on aspects of Buddhism or meditation. To join our email list, place an order or request a catalogue please visit our website at www.windhorsepublications.com or contact:

Windhorse Publications
38 Newmarket Road
Cambridge
CB5 8DT

Perseus Distribution
1094 Flex Drive
Jackson TN 38301
USA

Windhorse Books
PO Box 574
Newtown NSW 2042
Australia

About the FWBO

Windhorse Publications is an arm of the Friends of the Western Buddhist Order, which has more than sixty centres on five continents. Through these centres, members of the Western Buddhist Order offer regular programmes of events for the general public and for more experienced students. These include meditation classes, public talks, study on Buddhist themes and texts, and bodywork classes such as t'ai chi, yoga, and massage. The FWBO also runs several retreat centres and the Karuna Trust, a fundraising charity that supports social welfare projects in the slums and villages of Southern Asia.

Many FWBO centres have residential spiritual communities and ethical businesses associated with them. Arts activities are encouraged too, as is the development of strong bonds of friendship between people who share the same ideals. In this way the FWBO is developing a unique approach to Buddhism, not simply as a set of techniques, but as a creatively directed way of life for people in the modern world.

If you would like more information about the FWBO please visit the website at www.fwbo.org or write to:

London Buddhist Centre
51 Roman Road
London E2 0HU
UK

Arvaloka
14 Heartwood Circle
Newmarket NH 03857
USA

Sydney Buddhist Centre
24 Enmore Road
Sydney NSW 2042
Australia

Wildmind: A Step-by-Step Guide to Meditation

by Bodhipaksa

From how to build your own meditation stool to how a raisin can help you meditate, this illustrated guide explains everything you need to know to start or strengthen your meditation practice. This best-seller is in a new handy format and features brand new illustrations.

"Of great help to people interested in meditation and an inspiring reminder to those on the path."
- Joseph Goldstein, cofounder of the Insight Meditation Society and author of *One Dharma: The Emerging Western Buddhism*

"Bodhipaksa has written a beautiful and very accessible introduction to meditation. He guides us through all the basics of mindfulness and also loving-kindness meditations with the voice of a wise, kind, and patient friend."
- Dr. Lorne Ladner, author of *The Lost Art of Compassion*

ISBN 9781 899579 91 4
£11.99 / $18.95 / €15.95
264 pages

Why not try *A Buddhist View on...*?

Vegetarianism

by Bodhipaksa

How does what we eat affect us and our world? Is there a connection between vegetarianism and living a spiritual life? Doesn't HH the Dalai Lama eat meat?

A trained vet, respected teacher and happy vegan, Bodhipaksa answers all of these questions and more. Tackling issues such as genetically modified vegetables and modern ways of producing food he dispels widespread myths and reflects upon the diets dominant in the contemporary West. In comparison, he considers the diets of wandering monks in Ancient India and the diet of the Buddha himself.

By considering why people eat meat and relating this to Buddhist ethics he explores habits and the possibility of change. He takes a positive view of the benefits of vegetarianism, and shows practically, how to maintain a healthy and balanced vegan or vegetarian lifestyle.

This exploration shows how a meat-free life can not only lighten the body but also the soul.

ISBN 9781 899579 96 9
£7.99 / $13.95 / €9.95
104 pages

Saving the Earth

by Akuppa

If you been wondering how to make a difference in protecting the environment but didn't know where to start, this guide is the solution. Filled with practical tips as well as insightful reflections, Saving Earth provides tools for change while showing how the Buddhist philosophies of interconnectedness and compassion are of immense use in our efforts towards preserving the Earth.

ISBN 9781 899579 99 0
£7.99 / $13.95 / €9.95
152 pages